EMMA MAXWELL

Personal Taxes Made Easy

First edition

This book was professionally typeset on Reedsy.
Find out more at reedsy.com

Contents

Introduction

Did you know that the average American spends more on taxes than on food, clothing, and housing combined? It's a staggering reality that highlights the critical importance of understanding personal taxes. As a nation, we work hard to earn our income, yet far too many of us fail to take advantage of the legal strategies available to minimize our tax liabilities. This lack of knowledge not only hinders our ability to keep more of our hard-earned money but also prevents us from achieving the financial freedom we deserve.

That's where "Personal Taxes Made Easy" comes in. As a Certified Public Accountant with years of experience navigating the complex world of taxes and education, I've witnessed firsthand the transformative power of tax literacy. By demystifying the intricacies of personal taxes, this book aims to empower you with the knowledge and tools necessary to take control of your financial future.

Throughout these pages, we'll dive into the strategies and techniques that can help you legally reduce your tax burden. We'll explore often-overlooked tax concessions, uncover hidden deductions, and shed light on the most effective ways to structure your finances for optimal tax efficiency. Whether you're a salaried employee, a small business owner, or an investor, this book will provide you with actionable insights tailored to your unique situation.

But "Personal Taxes Made Easy" is more than just a guide to lowering your taxes. It's a road map to building lasting wealth and achieving financial independence. I'm not expecting you to be a tax guru at the end of this book, but if you manage to take one or two nuggets away, it will make an overall difference to how much money you take home versus give to Uncle Sam! By understanding how taxes impact your overall financial picture, you'll be better equipped to make informed decisions about saving, investing, and planning for your future. You'll discover how to integrate tax planning into your long-term financial strategy, ensuring that you're not just saving money today but setting yourself up for a prosperous tomorrow.

As we embark on this journey together, I encourage you to approach the material with an open mind and a willingness to learn. The concepts we'll cover may seem daunting at first and trust me first hand, tax is pretty boring! But I promise to break them down into easily digestible pieces. Each chapter is designed to build upon the previous one, gradually expanding your knowledge and confidence in navigating the tax landscape.

So, what will you gain from this book? Here are the key takeaways;

- Strategies to significantly reduce your tax liability without crossing any lines
- The truth about home office deductions and how to claim them without triggering an audit
- How to handle capital gains taxes and keep more of your investment profits
- Understanding the latest tax law changes that impact your filing this year
- The secret to ensuring you never miss out on tax credits you're entitled to
- How to manage taxes for your small business and claim all eligible deductions
- How to use budgeting apps and tools to streamline your tax preparation process
- The surprising tax benefits of contributing to an HSA and retirement accounts you might not know about
- How the "Buy, Borrow, Die" strategy works and why it might benefit you
- Choosing between standard and itemized deductions
- Real-life case studies that demonstrate successful tax strategies in action
- Practical tips for avoiding common tax filing mistakes that could cost you

Throughout the book, you'll find practical examples, real-life case studies, and step-by-step guidance to help you apply the concepts to your own situation. I invite you to take notes, complete the action steps, and refer back to the material as needed. The more actively you engage with the content, the more value you'll derive from it. I've tried hard to not make this book a snooze fest, which, given the topic,c could be likely, but something where you come away with more tools and knowledge than when you started.

This book is structured logically, starting with the basics and moving on to more advanced topics. Here's a brief overview of the chapters;

1. Foundations of Tax Literacy
2. Practical Tax Planning
3. Legal Tax Minimization Strategies
4. Navigating Complex Tax Scenarios
5. Real-Life Case Studies and Stories
6. Overcoming Tax Challenges and Fears
7. Building Long-Term Financial Strategies
8. Interactive Tools and Resources

Each chapter will end with specific, actionable steps you can take to improve your financial situation right away. You'll have a clear path to follow, making it easier to take control of your financial future.

I understand that taxes can be a source of stress and confusion for many people. Perhaps you've been putting off learning about taxes because it seems too complicated or overwhelming or, frankly, boring! Maybe you've been relying on a professional to handle your taxes without fully understanding the process. Whatever your starting point, know that you're not alone. By picking up this book, you've already taken a crucial first step towards empowering yourself and reclaiming control over your financial destiny.

So, let's dive in. Together, we'll demystify the world of personal taxes, unlock the strategies that can help you keep more of your hard-earned money, and pave the way for a brighter financial future. It's time to take charge of your taxes and start building the wealth you deserve.

Chapter 1

Foundations of Tax Literacy

You find yourself at a weekend barbecue, surrounded by friends and family, when the conversation inevitably turns to taxes. Amid the laughter and chatter, someone makes a joke about how no matter how much more money they earn, they always seem to end up with less in their bank account. Heads nod in agreement, and a few sighs of resignation echo through the group. It's a sentiment you might recognize—a common narrative that hints at the confusion surrounding tax brackets and the fear of losing more to the taxman with each raise or bonus. But what if I told you that understanding the tax bracket system could turn that sigh into a smile of relief and that the key to unlocking this knowledge is simpler than it seems?

1.1 Understanding Your Tax Bracket

The concept of tax brackets is foundational to tax literacy, yet it remains shrouded in mystery for many. Think of tax brackets as tiers within the broader progressive tax system, where your income is taxed in segments rather than as a whole. As you earn more, you progress through these brackets, with each bracket corresponding to a specific tax rate. For example, the first tier of

1

your income might be taxed at a lower rate, say 10%, while the next portion falls into a higher bracket, perhaps 12%, and so on. It's crucial to understand that only the income within each bracket is taxed at that bracket's rate, not your entire income. This distinction is vital because it counters the common misconception that moving into a higher tax bracket means all your income is taxed at the new, higher rate, potentially leaving you with less take-home pay. This fear often discourages people from seeking promotions or additional income streams, but it need not be a barrier to financial growth.

The progressive nature of this system ensures that higher income levels are taxed at progressively higher rates, but the structure is designed to be fair. Let's consider a case study: a single taxpayer versus a married couple filing jointly. According to the IRS's 2024 tax brackets, a single taxpayer might pay 10% on the first $11,600 of their income, 12% on the next $35,549, and so forth, while a married couple filing jointly pays these rates on doubled income thresholds (see table below).

Federal Income Tax Brackets for 2025 (filed by April 15, 2026)

	Single	Married Filing Jointly	Married Filing Separately	Head of Household
10%	$0 – $11,925	$0 – $23,850	$0 – $11,925	$0 – $17,000
12%	$11,925 – $48,475	$23,850 – $96,950	$11,925 – $48,475	$17,000 – $64,850
22%	$48,475 – $103,350	$96,950 – $206,700	$48,475 – $103,350	$64,850 – $103,350
24%	$103,350 – $197,300	$206,700 – $394,600	$103,350 – $197,300	$103,350 – $197,300
32%	$197,300 – $250,525	$394,600 – $501,050	$197,300 – $250,525	$197,300 – $250,500
35%	$250,525 – $626,350	$501,050 – $751,600	$250,525 – $375,800	$250,500 – $626,350
37%	$626,350+	$751,600+	$375,800+	$626,350+

This difference highlights how marital status can affect your tax situation, often leading to a lower overall tax rate for married couples. Understanding these brackets allows you to plan effectively, ensuring that you take advantage of the tax code's nuances rather than being overwhelmed by them. My suggestion is if you are married, do a return (but don't submit it) for both of your incomes and then do one each separately and see which delivers you the better outcome. The benefit of some of the tax apps we suggest in later chapters is that this is very easy to do.

One of the persistent myths about tax brackets is the fear of losing money by earning more. For instance, someone might hesitate to accept a raise because they believe it will push them into a higher tax bracket, resulting in a lower net income. However, this belief is unfounded. The truth is, only the portion of income that exceeds the previous bracket's threshold is taxed at the higher rate. Let's say you earn $48,000, placing you in the 22% bracket. Only the $849 above $47,151 is taxed at 22%, while the rest is taxed at the lower rates of 10% and 12%. This understanding helps dispel the myth that moving up a bracket is financially detrimental.

By grasping the mechanics of tax brackets, you arm yourself with the knowledge to navigate the tax landscape with confidence. This chapter sets the foundation for understanding how taxes work, not the scary monster we don't understand, but as a tool you can use to your advantage. Embrace this opportunity to transform your financial outlook, turning those barbecue conversations from frustration into empowerment. And seriously who wants to be talking about taxes at a barbecue anyway!

1.2 Demystifying Adjusted Gross Income (AGI)

In the realm of tax calculations, the term "Adjusted Gross Income," or AGI, often surfaces as a pivotal figure that demands attention. Think of AGI as the foundational layer upon which your tax liabilities are built. It's the magic number that determines not just how much tax you owe but also your eligibility for various deductions and credits. AGI is calculated by taking your total gross income—everything you earn from wages, investments, and other sources—and subtracting specific adjustments. These adjustments might include contributions to retirement accounts, student loan interest, or payments made to a Health Savings Account (HSA). Understanding AGI is crucial because it acts as a gatekeeper for many tax benefits that the government may pay you, influencing the amount of taxable income and thereby impacting the overall tax you pay.

Consider a scenario where two individuals, both earning the same gross income, end up with different AGI's due to varied adjustments. One might contribute to a traditional IRA, lowering their AGI, while the other might not take advantage of such opportunities, resulting in a higher AGI. This difference directly affects their taxable income, which is the portion of income subject to federal income tax after these deductions are taken off.

	Person 1	Person 2
Gross Income	80,000	80,000
Less Adjustments;		
Retirement Account contributions -	3,200	
HAS contributions -	2,000	
Student loan interest -	1,000	
Adjusted Gross Income	73,800	80,000

The significance of AGI becomes even clearer when you realize that it serves as the threshold for many tax benefits. For instance, certain deductions and credits are only available to those whose AGI falls below specified limits. The Child Tax Credit or the Earned Income Tax Credit (EITC) are prime examples where your AGI plays a decisive role. The Child Tax Credit is applicable to anyone earning $200,000 or less in Adjusted Gross Income or $400,000 if filing jointly. The Earned Income Tax Credit does differ depending on how many children you have and if you're filing jointly or on your own. Research these on the IRS website.

Lowering your AGI can be an effective strategy to enhance your tax efficiency, allowing you to qualify for more deductions and credits while reducing your overall tax liability. One practical approach is to increase contributions to retirement accounts. By putting more funds into a 401(k) or a traditional IRA, not only do you save for the future, but you also reduce your current AGI, which can lead to a lower tax bill. Similarly, contributions to an HSA can further lower your AGI, offering a triple tax advantage: Contributions are deductible, growth is tax-free, and withdrawals for qualified medical expenses are not taxed. Such contributions can be an astute decision, especially if you're looking to reduce your taxable income legally.

AGI's role in tax planning extends beyond just calculating your tax bill; it becomes a strategic tool for financial planning. For instance, if you plan to make charitable donations, understanding how these can affect your AGI is vital. Strategic charitable giving, particularly in years when your income might push your AGI to new thresholds, can provide dual benefits: supporting causes you care about while potentially lowering your taxable income. By understanding and managing your AGI, you gain more control over your financial landscape, making informed decisions that align with your broader financial goals.

The intricacies of AGI might seem daunting at first, but with careful planning and a clear understanding, it transforms from a mysterious figure into a powerful ally in your financial toolkit. Whether you're aiming to reduce your tax burden or increase eligibility for beneficial credits, AGI is a critical component of your tax strategy. By paying attention to the factors that influence it, you can effectively navigate the complexities of your tax situation, ensuring you make the most of the opportunities available to you.

1.3 Navigating Tax Filing Statuses

In the maze of tax preparation, choosing the correct filing status is like select-ing the right path to your destination—it sets the direction and determines the ease with which you navigate. The status you select influences not only the tax rates that apply to your income but also the deductions and credits you can claim, profoundly impacting your overall tax liability. Mainly, the IRS recognizes five filing statuses: single, married filing jointly, married filing separately, head of household, and qualifying widow(er). Each carries its own set of implications and benefits, tailored to fit various personal circumstances. The single status applies to those who are unmarried or legally separated, providing a straightforward option with fewer complications. For married couples, the choice between filing jointly or separately can significantly affect their tax outcomes. Filing jointly typically offers a lower tax rate and higher deductions, making it an attractive option for most couples. As you would have seen in the table in 1.1, filing as a married couple gives you double the tax bracket, so if you have one of you that earns more and one that earns less, you will get tax advantages to filing together. However, married filing separately might be beneficial if one spouse has substantial medical expenses or other deductions that could be limited by a higher combined income. It's a strategic decision that requires careful consideration of both parties' financial situations.

The head of household status is designed for single individuals who maintain a household for themselves and a qualifying dependent. This status provides a larger standard deduction and more favorable tax rates than filing as single, reflecting the additional financial responsibilities of caring for dependents. Qualifying widow(er) status is available to those who've lost a spouse within the last two years and have a dependent child, offering the same tax benefits as married filing jointly.

Choosing the right status involves a careful assessment of your life circum-stances, including relationships and dependents. Dual-income couples, for example, might benefit from running the numbers both jointly and separately to determine which option yields the best tax advantage. What you might find is that it may be different each year if you have started or stopped a job and earned less than the year before. Go to IRS Tax Withholding Estimator and run both scenarios quickly through. When I show you which tax software to choose, you can run them through this calculator too. Similarly, individuals with dependents should explore whether they qualify for head of household status, as it can offer significant tax savings.

Life events often necessitate changes in your filing status, making it essential to stay informed and adaptable. Marriage, divorce, the birth of a child, or the death of a spouse can all prompt a reevaluation of your tax situation. These events alter not only your personal circumstances but also your tax obligations and opportunities for deductions or credits. For instance, a couple marrying late in the year might find that filing jointly for that tax year provides immediate financial benefits due to the higher tax brackets available to married couples, while a divorce might lead each individual to file as single or head of household, depending on custody arrangements. Consider the scenario of divorced parents. If one parent has primary custody of the children, they may qualify for head of household status, which offers a larger standard deduction and lower tax rates. Meanwhile, the other parent, without the qualifying dependent, would file as single, potentially resulting in a higher tax bill. Understanding these distinctions and their implications can prevent unnecessary tax burdens and maximize potential refunds.

Navigating these statuses requires foresight and a clear understanding of how each option applies to your unique situation. It's not just about checking a box on a form; it's about aligning your tax approach with your life events and financial goals. By thoughtfully selecting your filing status, you set the stage for a tax strategy that supports your broader financial well-being.

1.4 The Basics of Tax Deductions and Credits

Understanding the distinction between tax deductions and credits is crucial for anyone looking to reduce their tax liability effectively. In simple terms, tax deductions lower your taxable income, which can reduce the amount of tax you owe. For instance, if your taxable income is $50,000 and you have $5,000 in deductions, your taxable income drops to $45,000. This reduction lowers the amount of your income subject to tax, potentially shifting you to a lower tax bracket. On the other hand, tax credits reduce your tax bill directly, dollar for dollar. If you owe $1,000 in taxes but have a $500 tax credit, your tax bill decreases to $500. Both deductions and credits are vital tools in tax planning, each playing a unique role in reducing tax liability. By leveraging them effectively, you can ensure that you're not paying more taxes than necessary.

Several common deductions and credits can significantly impact your tax return, yet many taxpayers overlook them. The home mortgage interest deduction, for example, allows homeowners to deduct the interest paid on mortgage loans, lowering taxable income. This deduction provides substantial savings, especially in the early years of a mortgage when interest payments are higher. Another valuable credit is the Child Tax Credit, which offers financial relief to families with dependent children. This credit not only reduces tax liability but can also result in a refund if it exceeds the amount of taxes owed. To claim these benefits, it's essential to maintain accurate records and understand the eligibility criteria. Many taxpayers miss out on these savings simply because they aren't aware of them or don't know how to claim them effectively.

The most common tax deductions are;

- Student loan interest payments
- Education expenses directly related to your job
- Self-employed health insurance payments
- Mortgage interest if you own your own house (as well as for investment properties)
- Contributions to retirement accounts
- Some alimony payments
- Medical expenses (these will need to exceed 7.5% of your gross income)
- Health Savings Account contributions
- State and local tax deductions
- Home office deduction
- Charitable giving
- Business expenses if you run your own business or are a freelancer

The most common tax credits are;

- Earned Income tax credit for low to middle-income earners
- Premium tax credit for out-of-pocket health insurance premiums
- Child tax credit
- Child and dependent care credit
- Adoption credit
- Retirement Savings contribution credit
- American opportunity tax credit for college students
- Lifetime learning credit
- Residential energy credits for both your principal place of residence and investment properties
- Electric vehicle tax credit

For a full list of credits and deductions, see the Credit and deductions link in the references section.

Maximizing your deductions and credits requires a strategic approach. One of the first decisions you'll face is whether to take the standard deduction, which is a standard amount per person, or to itemize. The standard deduction is a fixed amount determined by your filing status and provides a straight-forward way to reduce taxable income. At the time of writing, the standard deduction for single or married filing separately is $14,600, for married couple filing jointly $29,200 and $21,900 for head of household. However, if your total qualifying expenses exceed the standard deduction, itemizing may be more beneficial. This involves listing each deduction separately, which can include medical expenses, state and local taxes, and charitable contributions. It's crucial to weigh the pros and cons of each option to determine which provides the greater tax advantage. For some, itemizing can lead to a significantly lower tax bill, while for others, the standard deduction may suffice.

Incorporating deductions and credits into your broader financial strategy can enhance your overall tax efficiency. By understanding how they affect your effective tax rate, you can plan better for the future. The effective tax rate is the average rate at which your income is taxed, taking into account all deductions and credits. By reducing your effective tax rate through the strategic use of deductions and credits, you retain more of your income, allowing for increased savings and investment opportunities. This approach not only helps in the current tax year but can also have long-term benefits. By consistently reducing tax liability, you can redirect funds toward achieving financial goals, such as retirement savings or paying down debt.

So now you've seen this full list of deductions and credits, you realize you haven't been claiming what you're entitled to. Can you go back and re-submit your tax returns? The short answer is yes. You have three years from the date you filed your return or 2 years after you paid your tax/received our refund. If you filed electronically, you can re-submit electronically too, otherwise, you can file a Form 1040-X Amended US Individual Income Tax Return for an individual.

To navigate this landscape effectively, it's beneficial to develop a methodical approach to identifying and claiming deductions and credits. Start by keeping meticulous records of all potential deductible expenses and credits throughout the year. Consider consulting resources like the IRS guidelines or a tax professional to ensure you're not missing out on any opportunities. Additionally, regularly reviewing your financial situation can reveal new opportunities for deductions and credits, especially as tax laws evolve. With the right strategies in place, you can transform what might seem like a daunting task into a rewarding exercise in financial empowerment.

1.5 Common Misconceptions About Taxes

Stepping into the world of taxes, you might find yourself surrounded by a fog of myths and misconceptions that can lead you astray. These misunderstandings often become entrenched in our minds, shaping the way we approach tax season and ultimately affecting our financial decisions. One of the most prevalent myths concerns audits. Many people live in constant fear of the dreaded IRS audit, believing it to be a common occurrence that hangs over every tax return like a dark cloud. In reality, audits are relatively rare, especially for those who file accurately and transparently. The IRS selects returns for audits based on several factors, including discrepancies and potential red flags, but the overall audit rate is quite low. This unfounded fear often drives taxpayers to overpay or make hasty decisions just to avoid attracting attention. By understanding the actual audit process and criteria, you can approach your taxes with confidence rather than dread.

Another common area of confusion involves tax deadlines. Many taxpayers mistakenly believe that if they miss the April filing deadline, they're automatically doomed to face severe penalties. While it's true that missing the deadline can result in fines, there are often options available, such as filing for an extension. However, an extension only grants more time to file, not to pay any taxes owed. This distinction is crucial. If you're unable to pay your full tax bill by the deadline, the IRS offers installment plans that help manage the financial burden without incurring excessive penalties. Understanding these nuances can alleviate unnecessary stress and prevent financial pitfalls.

Misinterpretations also extend to tax refund processes. Some taxpayers think that receiving a large refund is a sign of financial acumen or a reward, when in fact, it often means they've overpaid their taxes throughout the year. A large refund means you've essentially given the government an interest-free loan of your money. Adjusting your withholding to more accurately match your tax liability can result in more take-home pay throughout the year, giving you greater control over your cash flow. On the flip side, owing money at tax time isn't necessarily a bad thing if it means you've kept more of your money during the year.

Believing in these myths can lead to poor financial decisions and missed opportunities. The unnecessary fear of audits, for instance, might lead someone to hire expensive tax services they don't need, while misunderstanding deadlines can result in avoidable penalties. These misconceptions can create a cycle of stress and financial inefficiency, making tax season more daunting than it should be. By tackling these myths head-on, you can transform your approach to taxes from one of trepidation to one of empowerment.

To combat these myths, proactive tax education is key. Engaging with reliable resources and staying informed about tax laws and processes can prevent misinformation from taking root. Look, I'm not asking you to become a tax nerd, but it is helpful to keep informed. Rather than scroll through the daunting IRS website for tax updates (snooze!!), try subscribing to TurboTax or TaxSlayer newsletter updates, where they will let clients know the latest changes. Also, if filing through an accountant, they should do this as well, just ask. The IRS website is a valuable source of accurate information, offering resources and tools to clarify tax processes and answer common questions. Books, webinars, and courses by tax professionals can also provide insights and updates on the latest tax developments. By actively seeking out this information, you can build a solid foundation of tax knowledge that will serve you well year after year.

Cultivating an informed perspective on taxes not only helps dispel myths but also enhances your overall financial literacy. The more you understand how taxes work, the better equipped you are to make decisions that align with your financial goals. This proactive approach transforms tax season from a dreaded obligation into an opportunity to optimize your finances. Through continuous learning and engagement, you can navigate the tax landscape with clarity and confidence, leaving misconceptions and myths behind.

1.6 Overcoming Tax Preparation Anxiety

The mere thought of tax season can stir up feelings of dread and anxiety for many. It's a common reaction, one that evokes visions of towering piles of paperwork, complex forms, and the omnipresent fear of making a costly mistake. This anxiety is not unfounded; the process of filing taxes can seem overwhelming, especially when faced with the intricacies of the tax code. Psychological barriers often exacerbate these feelings, with thoughts of procrastination, self-doubt, and confusion clouding the task at hand. The good news is that you're not alone in these feelings, and there are ways to tackle them effectively, turning tax preparation from a daunting task into a manageable one.

Start by organizing your financial documents early. This simple step can significantly reduce stress as deadlines approach. Gather all necessary paperwork, such as W-2s, 1099s, receipts for deductible expenses, and any other relevant financial records. Consider setting up a dedicated folder or digital storage system, categorizing documents by type and year. This organization not only simplifies the preparation process but also ensures that you have everything you need when it's time to file, preventing last-minute scrambles and forgotten forms.

During the year, I just put any information I have into my tax folder and then into a spreadsheet. There are free copies included in the references section - Tax Expense spreadsheet. Then, when I'm ready to file, I can just input the numbers from my spreadsheet straight into the tax software I use, or you can send this to your accountant if you're getting them to file for you. Don't be that person who turns up to your accountant's office with a shoebox full of receipts. They charge by the hour, so the less prepared you are, the more hours they have to work to prepare your tax return and the more you'll get charged. Utilizing tax software can also be a game-changer in managing preparation anxiety. Modern tax software is designed to guide you through the filing process step- by- step, often with user-friendly interfaces and helpful tips along the way. It can automatically import information from previous years, calculate deductions and credits, and even check for errors before submission. Many programs also offer intuitive question-and-answer formats, simulating the experience of sitting down with a tax professional. By leveraging these tools, you can simplify the filing process, save time, and feel confident that your return is accurate and complete. Try TurboTax and TaxSlayer.

Beginning your tax preparation early in the year provides numerous advantages. Early preparation allows you to identify any missing documents or information well before the deadline, giving you ample time to address any issues that arise. It also reduces the pressure and stress associated with the looming April deadline, allowing you to approach the process with a clear mind and a steady hand. Creating a tax calendar can further enhance this approach, with reminders set for key dates, such as when to gather documents, when to start using software, and the filing deadline itself. This proactive strategy transforms tax season into a series of manageable steps rather than a single, insurmountable task.

For some, the idea of tackling taxes alone remains anxiety-inducing, even with these strategies in place. In such cases, hiring a tax professional can significantly ease the burden. A qualified tax advisor can provide personalized guidance tailored to your unique financial situation, ensuring that all deductions and credits are maximized while minimizing the risk of errors. When choosing a tax advisor, look for someone with the appropriate credentials and experience, such as a CPA or an enrolled agent. Seek recommendations from friends or family, or read reviews to find a professional who communicates clearly and addresses your specific needs. This investment in expert assistance can offer peace of mind, allowing you to focus on other aspects of your financial planning. Try searching in your postcode and state at https://irs.treasury.gov/rpo/rpo.jsf. If you're a freelancer or small business owner, try and find someone that specializes in that field by speaking with them on the phone.

The benefit of using a tax professional is that they should be able to claim deductions and minimize your tax liability, so that the fee they charge should more than cover the benefit you get in your tax return. If you've never done your own taxes before, I do suggest hiring a tax professional, at least initially, as they will be able to file your taxes more efficiently than you and will ask you questions to prompt what deductions and credits will apply to you. If next year your situation has not changed, you can file by yourself if you like and just copy what they did last year and input the new numbers for this year's return. If your situation changes, like you got divorced or your kids are no longer dependents, then it might be worth getting them to have a look at helping you file that year. Hopefully, you're now better educated about the deductions and credits available to you.

Addressing tax preparation anxiety involves acknowledging the stress it can cause and taking steps to mitigate it. By organizing your documents, utilizing effective tools, planning ahead, and enlisting professional help when needed, you can transform the tax preparation process from a source of anxiety into an opportunity for financial empowerment. As you approach each tax season with newfound confidence, the task becomes not just a chore to check off your list but an integral part of managing your financial health.

OK, remember I said at the end of each chapter there would be actionable steps you'd need to do in order to cement the learning from this chapter in place, so here goes.

Don't move on to the next chapter without doing the following;

1. Calculate your Adjust Gross Income (AGI). You can find this in your online account on the IRS website, or you can enter it into your tax software. Try TaxSlayer or TurboTax

2. Could you adjust your AGI to enable you to claim tax benefits you're not currently receiving? What will that do to your take-home pay if you make these deductions? Go to IRS Tax Withholding Estimator to check the differences in both scenarios

3. Do you know your tax filing status? Run each scenario through the IRS Tax Withholding Estimator to see which gives you a better outcome

4. Are there some deductions and credits you're not claiming that you should? Do you need to contact your HR department and start some HSA and retirement contributions?

5. Do you need to re-file any prior years' tax returns? If you're adding credits and deductions that you've missed, it will be worth it to re-file as you'll get a refund, so it could be worth the effort and may be faster than you think. So come on, go ahead and do it now!

6. Have you set up a dedicated tax folder and spreadsheet? Do that now if you're partway through a tax year and gather all the information you'll need for that tax year

7. Will you need tax software to manage your return, or can you use IRS Free File? Go and have a look at TurboTax and TaxSlayer as well as IRS Free File and choose one that suits you

8. Have you decided whether you will file by yourself or employ a tax professional? If you are an individual and your return is not complex,

you should be able to file using tax software, but if your return is more complicated and you own investment properties or have secondary income, a CPA can prove invaluable. Go to https://irs.treasury.gov/rpo/rpo.jsf to find one in your state and post code

Wow, this chapter was a lot! This is by far the longest chapter with the most action steps, so I hope I haven't lost you along the way. Don't be overwhelmed with all this information; just methodically go through each of the steps and cross each of them off your list. It's a marathon, not a sprint. You're doing great!

Chapter 2

Practical Tax Planning

Picture yourself at the start of a new year, not just with resolutions to improve your health or career but with a commitment to mastering your taxes. For many, taxes are a once-a-year hassle, a furious scramble to gather documents and decipher forms. But what if tax planning were as routine as your morning coffee, a process integrated into your life year-round? This chapter is about transforming tax planning from a seasonal headache into a steady, manageable part of your financial strategy. By proactively planning throughout the year, you not only alleviate the stress that peaks as April approaches but also position yourself to capitalize on opportunities that can reduce your tax burden and enhance your financial health.

The benefits of proactive tax planning are clear. By avoiding the last-minute rush, you can approach tax season with confidence and clarity rather than anxiety and uncertainty. Imagine having everything in place well before the deadline—documents organized, deductions maximized, and credits claimed. This preparation not only saves time but also enhances accuracy, reducing the risk of costly errors. Proactive planning also allows you to make informed decisions that can positively impact your tax situation, such as adjusting your withholdings to better match your liability and prevent large refunds or unexpected bills. By treating tax planning as a continuous process, you can navigate the complexities of the tax code with ease and assurance.

Year-round tax preparedness begins with regular reviews of your financial documents, such as your pay stubs. These reviews ensure that your withholdings align with your expected tax liability, preventing surprises when you file your return. If you notice discrepancies or changes in your financial situation, such as a raise or an unexpected bonus, it's wise to adjust your withholdings accordingly. This adjustment ensures that you neither overpay nor underpay your taxes throughout the year, keeping your budget on track and your finances stable. It's a small step, but one that significantly impacts your overall tax strategy.

Another critical component of effective tax planning is tracking life changes that can influence your taxes. Major events, like starting a new job, getting married, or welcoming a child, can alter your tax situation dramatically. A new job might affect your tax bracket or eligibility for certain deductions, while a change in marital status could open up new filing options. The birth of a child brings potential for additional credits and deductions, like the Child Tax Credit, that can reduce your tax liability. By staying attuned to these changes and understanding their implications, you can adjust your tax strategy to reflect your current circumstances and maximize your savings.

Incorporating tools and resources into your tax planning routine can streamline the process and enhance your efficiency. Budgeting apps, for example, help you track income and expenses, providing a clear picture of your financial landscape and identifying areas for potential tax savings. Try Empower, YNAB (You Need a Budget), or Every Dollar. They link to your bank account, and all have great visual dashboards. Tax filing software offers guidance and support, simplifying the complexities of filing and ensuring compliance with current tax laws. These tools not only save time but also empower you to take control of your financial situation, transforming tax planning from a daunting task into a manageable and even empowering activity. Try CashApp taxes, which is free, or TaxSlayer, which has guidance along the way, and you can pay an additional fee to have an expert guide you if needed.

Exercise: Building Your Tax Toolkit

Think about the tools that could enhance your tax planning efforts. Are there budgeting apps that align with your financial habits? Perhaps a tax software that simplifies filing? Create a list of potential tools, then research their features and benefits to determine which best fits your needs. Once selected, incorporate them into your routine and monitor their impact on your tax planning process.

By embracing these strategies and resources, you lay the groundwork for a proactive approach to tax planning that supports your financial goals. This shift in perspective not only alleviates the stress of tax season but also empowers you to navigate the complexities of your finances with confidence and clarity.

2.1 Developing a Tax-Efficient Investment Strategy

Imagine your investments as a well-tended garden, where each plant is carefully chosen and placed to ensure optimal growth and yield. In the realm of investing, asset allocation plays a similar role, guiding you to minimize tax burdens while maximizing returns. The way you allocate your assets can significantly impact your tax efficiency. For instance, placing bonds in tax-deferred accounts like a traditional IRA or a 401(k) shields the interest income from immediate taxes. This strategy is particularly effective because bond income is generally taxed at higher rates than capital gains. By deferring these taxes, you allow your investments to grow tax-free.

Within this framework, mutual funds and Exchange-Traded Funds (ETFs) emerge as crucial tools designed to reduce taxable distributions. Their structure often leads to fewer taxable events, particularly when they employ a low turnover rate. This is where index funds shine, as they typically involve minimal trading, thereby generating fewer capital gains. The result? A smoother tax experience. When you choose funds with low turnover, you effectively reduce the frequency and impact of taxable distributions. This approach not only benefits your tax bill but also aligns with a long-term investment strategy, letting your assets grow with minimal interference. What does this mean in plain English? Because you are selling less often, it doesn't trigger a taxable event, but the reality is if you are selling more often, you're likely making a profit. If you're making a profit, then you'll pay tax; it's as simple as that!

Tax-loss harvesting is another powerful technique in your tax efficiency toolkit. It involves selling investments at a loss to offset gains elsewhere in your portfolio. By strategically realizing these losses, you can reduce your taxable income, potentially saving a significant amount in taxes. This strategy requires careful timing and a keen understanding of the wash sale rule, which disallows a loss deduction if you repurchase the same or a substantially identical security within 30 days. By adhering to these guidelines, you can effectively use losses as a tool to manage your tax liabilities. I'm not suggesting you lose money for the sake of losing money, but if your portfolio has a loss-making investment and you were going to offload it anyway, then you could time it and sell it to offset against a gain to pay zero or minimal tax.

Choosing the right accounts for your investments is akin to selecting the ideal soil for your garden. Each account type offers different tax advantages, and understanding these can guide your investment decisions. A Roth IRA, for example, allows your investments to grow tax-free, with tax-free withdrawals during retirement. This can be particularly advantageous if you anticipate being in a higher tax bracket in the future. On the other hand, a traditional IRA offers upfront tax deductions on contributions, deferring taxes until withdrawal. Your choice between these accounts should reflect your current tax situation and future expectations, ensuring your investments are well-positioned to thrive. Get tax advice before you set this up, as it can have ramifications for your overall wealth.

Incorporating these strategies requires a thoughtful approach, balancing immediate tax benefits with long-term growth potential. Consider your overall financial picture and future goals when making decisions about asset allocation and account selection. By doing so, you not only enhance the efficiency of your investments but also lay a solid foundation for financial stability. This tax-efficient approach to investing empowers you to maximize returns while keeping tax liabilities in check, providing the peace of mind that your financial garden is growing as productively as possible.

2.2 Tax Implications of Retirement Contributions

When you contribute to retirement accounts, you're not just saving for the future—you're also taking advantage of significant tax benefits today. Let's explore how different retirement accounts can impact your taxable income and retirement savings, starting with the 401(k). Contributions to a 401(k) are made with pre-tax dollars, meaning they reduce your taxable income for the year. This reduction can be substantial, lowering your overall tax bill and allowing you to save more money upfront. Over time, these contributions grow tax-deferred, meaning you won't pay taxes on the earnings until you withdraw them in retirement. This deferral can lead to significant growth, as the funds compound without the drag of annual taxes. The 401(k) becomes not just a savings tool but a powerful tax strategy that benefits you both now and later.

As you consider Individual Retirement Accounts (IRAs), you'll encounter two main types: Roth and Traditional. Each offers unique tax advantages, depending on your current situation and future expectations. Contributions to a Traditional IRA are similar to a 401(k), made with pre-tax dollars, which lowers your taxable income in the year you contribute. The funds then grow tax-deferred, with taxes due upon withdrawal. In contrast, a Roth IRA operates differently. You contribute with after-tax dollars, so there's no immediate tax break. However, the real benefit comes later: withdrawals in retirement are tax-free. This can be especially beneficial if you expect to be in a higher tax bracket when you retire. The choice between a Roth and a Traditional IRA hinges on anticipating your future tax situation and deciding whether you prefer tax savings now or in the years to come.

Understanding contribution limits is crucial to maximizing the benefits of these accounts. For 2024, the IRS sets the limit for IRA contributions at

$7,000 per year, with an additional $1,000 allowed for those aged 50 and over, known as catch-up contributions. For 401(k) plans, the contribution limit is $23,000, with a catch-up contribution of $7,500 for those over 50. Exceeding these limits can lead to penalties, so it's vital to monitor your contributions closely. Catch-up contributions offer a valuable opportunity for those nearing retirement to boost their savings significantly. If you find yourself in this age bracket, consider maximizing these contributions to enhance your retirement nest egg, taking full advantage of the tax benefits available to you.

Strategies for maximizing retirement contributions often involve careful planning and keeping a keen eye on your financial landscape. One approach is to increase your contributions gradually, aligning them with salary increases or bonuses. This method ensures that you're consistently building your retirement savings without feeling the pinch in your day-to-day budget. Another tactic is to automate your contributions, setting them to increase automatically each year. Automation ensures that your savings grow steadily, taking advantage of compounding interest over time. Additionally, if your employer offers a matching program, strive to contribute enough to receive the full match—it's essentially free money that boosts your retirement savings and enhances your financial security.

Retirement accounts are a cornerstone of financial planning, offering a blend of immediate tax advantages and long-term growth potential. Whether you're just starting your career or approaching retirement, understanding the tax implications of your contributions is essential to making informed decisions that align with your goals. By strategically utilizing these accounts, you can reduce your tax liability today while building a secure financial future for yourself and your loved ones. As you navigate the complexities of retirement planning, remember that your contributions are more than just numbers— they're a foundation for the life you envision in the years to come. You can't rely solely on Social Security to fund the retirement of your dreams.

2.3 Home Office Deductions Simplified

In today's world, where remote work has become the norm for many, understanding the specifics of home office deductions can lead to substantial tax savings. To qualify for the home office deduction, the IRS mandates that the space you claim must be used exclusively and regularly for your business. This means that the area should not double up as a guest room or play area when not in use for work. The exclusivity requirement ensures that the space is dedicated to business activities, setting clear boundaries between your professional and personal life. Regular use, on the other hand, implies a consistent pattern of work, as opposed to an occasional or sporadic use. This criterion helps establish the legitimacy of the claim, ensuring that the deduction reflects genuine business needs. My view is if there's a desk there and you work from that space, then it's a deduction!

When it comes to calculating the home office deduction, you have two methods to choose from: the simplified method and the regular method. Each has its pros and cons, and the choice often boils down to personal preference and the specifics of your situation. The simplified method offers ease and convenience, allowing you to deduct $5 per square foot of your home office, up to a maximum of 300 square feet. This straightforward calculation requires minimal paperwork and record-keeping, making it an attractive option for those who prefer simplicity. It also eliminates the need to track actual expenses, which can be a relief for many. However, the downside is that this method may not yield as high a deduction as the regular method, especially if your actual expenses are significant.

The regular method, by contrast, involves a more detailed approach, requiring you to calculate the actual expenses associated with your home office. This includes a portion of mortgage interest or rent, utilities, insurance, and depreciation of the square meterage office space. While this method demands meticulous record-keeping and a more complex calculation process, it can result in a larger deduction if your home office expenses are substantial. For those willing to invest the time and effort, the regular method can provide a more accurate reflection of the costs involved in maintaining a home office. However, it requires ongoing tracking and documentation, which might not be feasible for everyone. For individuals working from home for an employer, you fill out a Form 8829. For those running their own business, you fill out Schedule C.

Common deductible expenses for home offices include;

- Rent
- Mortgage interest if you own your home (not the principal)
- Utilities
- Homeowners insurance
- House cleaning
- Pest control
- Home security
- Internet
- Depreciation of your home (if you own it)

The above deductions get allocated based on the square meterage (sqm) of your office space, for instance, if your house is 1,00 sqm and your office space is 100 sqm, then you can claim 10% of the above costs. If you have something that is 100% for your home office, like lighting or a dedicated phone or internet line, then that is 100% deductible. These deductions recognize the costs associated with maintaining a professional workspace within your home, providing tax relief that aligns with actual business expenses.

Despite the potential for tax savings, it's essential to avoid common mistakes that could trigger an audit. One frequent error is mixing personal and business expenses, which can complicate your tax return and raise red flags with the IRS. To prevent this, maintain separate records for your business and personal expenses, ensuring clear documentation of all deductions claimed. Another pitfall is claiming a space that does not meet the exclusivity requirement, such as a dining room table or a shared family area. Missteps like these can undermine the legitimacy of your claim, leading to complications and potential penalties. By adhering to IRS guidelines and maintaining thorough records, you can confidently take advantage of the home office deduction, enhancing your financial efficiency while supporting your professional endeavors.

2.4 Strategic Timing of Income and Expenses

Imagine having the power to influence how much tax you pay, not by earning less, but by strategically timing when you receive income or incur expenses. This concept might seem foreign, yet it's a savvy approach to managing your tax liabilities effectively. By shifting income to a year when you're in a lower tax bracket, you can significantly reduce the taxes you owe. This strategy is particularly useful if you anticipate a year with reduced income, such as taking a sabbatical or transitioning to part-time work. By deferring income, like delaying a year-end bonus to the following year, you ensure it coincides with a lower tax bracket, reducing your immediate tax burden. This approach allows you to keep more of what you earn, providing financial flexibility and peace of mind.

Let's consider some practical examples. Imagine you're set to receive a substantial bonus at the end of December. If you expect your income to decrease the following year, you could negotiate with your employer to delay the bonus until January. This simple shift could place you in a lower tax bracket, resulting in a smaller tax bill. Similarly, if you're selling a property, using an installment sale can spread the income over several years. This strategy prevents a significant spike in your taxable income in the year of sale, smoothing it out over time and potentially lowering your tax rate. These tactics require foresight and planning but offer tangible rewards when executed correctly. Weight up the cash flow delay versus the tax saving.

Timing isn't just about income; it extends to expenses as well. In high-income years, accelerating deductible expenses can enhance your tax efficiency. Consider prepaying mortgage interest or making charitable contributions before the year's end. These actions can increase your itemized deductions, allowing you to exceed the standard deduction and reduce your taxable income. This approach is particularly beneficial if you expect your income to decrease in the near future, as maximizing deductions when they offer the greatest benefit can lead to significant savings. To enable this to happen, you would physically need the cash to leave your bank account, so ensure you understand the cash flow impact. By strategically managing both income and expenses, you create a balanced approach to tax planning that aligns with your financial goals.

Understanding and utilizing tax brackets effectively can further refine your strategy. Tax brackets determine the rate at which your income is taxed, and by planning around these brackets, you can optimize your tax situation. For example, bunching itemized deductions into a single year can push you over the standard deduction threshold, enabling you to itemize when it provides the most advantage. This might involve grouping medical expenses, charitable contributions, and other deductions into one year rather than spreading them across multiple years. Such strategic planning allows you to maximize your tax savings by taking full advantage of the tax code's nuances. Again, this is all about timing your deductions and is available if this applies to you.

By integrating these timing strategies into your financial planning, you not only enhance your tax efficiency but also align your tax liabilities with your broader financial picture. This proactive approach transforms tax planning from a reactive task into a strategic component of your financial management, empowering you to make informed decisions that support your long-term objectives. As you consider these strategies, reflect on your current financial situation and future expectations. Are there opportunities to shift income or expenses in a way that aligns with your goals? By exploring these possibilities, you open new avenues for financial efficiency and success, making the most of the resources and opportunities available to you.

2.5 Implementing a Tax Calendar for Success

Imagine a world where tax season doesn't sneak up on you like an uninvited guest. A tax calendar can transform that vision into reality, serving as your road map through the intricate landscape of tax planning and preparation. By organizing important dates and deadlines, a tax calendar helps ensure that nothing slips through the cracks, providing a structured approach to managing your tax responsibilities. The importance of adhering to these deadlines cannot be overstated—missing them can result in penalties and additional stress, whereas meeting them ensures a smoother, more predictable tax experience.

A well-constructed tax calendar includes a variety of key dates and activities designed to keep your tax obligations on track. For instance, if you make estimated tax payments, you'll want to note the quarterly due dates: April 15, June 15, September 15, and January 15 of the following year. These payments are crucial for those with income not subject to withholding, such as freelancers or business owners, ensuring that they stay in compliance with the IRS's pay-as-you-go tax system. Additionally, if you're contributing to an IRA, it's important to remember that contributions for the current tax year can be made up until April 15 of the following year. This deadline provides an opportunity to maximize your retirement savings while strategically managing your taxable income.

To create a personalized tax calendar, consider leveraging digital tools that simplify the process. Many calendar apps, such as Google Calendar or Apple's iCal, allow you to set reminders for critical dates. These reminders can be scheduled to alert you days or even weeks in advance, giving you ample time to prepare. For a more integrated approach, the IRS offers an online tax calendar that provides timely updates and alerts for various tax-related activities. This resource is especially useful for small business owners, offering insights into specific deposit and filing deadlines relevant to their operations. By synchronizing these tools with your existing calendar, you can streamline your tax planning efforts, reducing the risk of oversight.

The benefits of maintaining a tax calendar extend beyond mere convenience. By keeping all your tax-related activities and deadlines organized in one place, you significantly reduce the likelihood of errors and missed payments. This organization helps avoid the last-minute rush often associated with tax season, where the pressure to file on time can lead to mistakes. Instead, a tax calendar allows you to approach each task methodically, ensuring that nothing is overlooked. This proactive approach not only saves time and stress but also fosters a sense of control over your financial affairs, as you're able to address each obligation with confidence and clarity.

Consider the peace of mind that comes with having a reliable system in place to manage your tax responsibilities. With a tax calendar guiding your actions, you can focus on optimizing your tax strategy rather than scrambling to meet deadlines. This shift in perspective transforms tax planning from a reactive chore into a proactive opportunity, empowering you to make informed decisions that align with your financial goals. The calendar becomes more than just a list of dates; it evolves into a foundational tool that supports your long-term financial well-being.

As we conclude this chapter, take a moment to reflect on how these practical tax strategies can enhance your financial management. By integrating these approaches into your routine, you not only streamline the tax process but also set the stage for greater fiscal health. With a clear plan in place, you're better equipped to navigate the complexities of personal taxes, ensuring that your financial journey is as smooth and successful as possible.

Don't move on to the next chapter without doing the following;

1. Do you have all your documents in one place? Pick the best storage system for you, whether it's printing everything and inputting it into a spreadsheet or inputting it online. Choose how you will store your documents and get busy getting organized!
2. Have you set up a budgeting app? Check out Empower, YNAB, or EveryDollar and create a login and link your accounts
3. Have you chosen tax filing software? Check our Cash App Taxes or

TaxSlayer

4. Do you need to think about selling some of your investments to get you in a better tax position by year end? Do some planning

5. Do you need to change or do a top-up retirement contribution? Plan which tax year you will do this in

6. Have you decided whether you will be claiming a home office deduction? Which method will you use? Do the math on both methods to see which one is better for you

7. Can you, and do you want to strategically spread your income and expenses over multiple tax years?

8. Add key tax dates to your calendar to ensure you get your tax filing done by the due dates. You don't want to miss these and get unnecessary penalties and be a target for an IRS audit

Chapter 3

Legal Tax Minimization Strategies

Imagine standing on the edge of a vast sea, one that promises endless opportunities but also harbors hidden complexities beneath its surface. This sea is much like the world of taxes—expansive and full of potential for those who know where to navigate. Legal tax minimization is your compass, guiding you through this financial expanse by showing how to reduce your tax liabilities within the boundaries of the law. What does this mean in simple English, you might ask? Tax minimization, in its simplest explanation, means not paying any more tax than you need to. Unlike tax evasion, which skirts legality and risks severe penalties, tax minimization involves using available laws and resources to your advantage. It's about understanding the options, like deductions, credits, and strategic financial planning, that can substantially lower what you owe each year. That's more money in your wallet, cool huh!

Delving into tax minimization requires a clear distinction between tax avoidance and tax evasion. Tax avoidance is completely legal and involves arranging your finances to pay the least amount of tax possible. This might involve investing in retirement accounts or making charitable contributions, which not only benefit you but also align with ethical conduct. On the contrary, tax evasion is illegal and involves deceitful practices like under-reporting income or inflating deductions. The IRS scrutinizes such fraudulent activities closely, and the penalties can be severe, including fines or imprisonment. Understanding this distinction is crucial to ensuring your strategies remain above board and within the scope of the law.

The benefits of strategic tax minimization extend beyond mere compliance. It can significantly enhance your disposable income, giving you more flexibility to invest, save, or spend as you see fit. By keeping more of your earnings, you're able to channel funds into other financial goals, whether that's building an emergency fund, paying down debt, or investing in opportunities that promise future growth. This financial breathing room is invaluable, allowing you to improve your quality of life or prepare more effectively for unforeseen expenses.

However, as with any powerful tool, ethical considerations must remain at the forefront of tax planning. While it might be tempting to push the boundaries for greater savings, maintaining ethical standards ensures that your financial practices are sustainable and aligned with societal values. Overly aggressive tax schemes can attract unwanted attention from tax authorities and damage your financial reputation. Engaging in ethical tax planning fosters trust and accountability, both with the IRS and within your community. It also sets a positive example for others, demonstrating that success need not come at the expense of integrity.

As you progress through this chapter, you'll encounter various strategies designed to help you legally minimize your taxes. From leveraging retirement accounts to utilizing charitable contributions, each method is crafted to enhance your financial position while adhering to ethical guidelines. The upcoming sections will delve into specific tactics, offering detailed insights and practical advice on how to implement them effectively. This foundation is not just about understanding the mechanics of tax minimization but about building a comprehensive strategy that aligns with your financial goals.

To help visualize these concepts, consider reflecting on your current financial strategies. How might they be adjusted to incorporate these tax minimization techniques? What ethical standards do you prioritize in your financial planning, and how can they guide your approach? By contemplating these questions, you prepare yourself to engage with the material actively and thoughtfully, setting the stage for deeper understanding and more informed decision-making.

3.1 The "Buy, Borrow, Die" Strategy

Imagine you're an artist with a blank canvas, each brushstroke representing a decision in your financial life. Now, picture this canvas evolving over time, accumulating value, and transforming into a masterpiece. The "Buy, Borrow, Die" strategy paints a similar picture in the realm of tax planning. It's a method primarily embraced by the affluent to minimize taxes while simultaneously building wealth. At its core, this strategy revolves around purchasing appreciating assets such as real estate or stocks. These assets are akin to your masterpiece—growing in value over time without being sold, thus avoiding capital gains tax. This tactic hinges on the understanding that as long as the asset remains unsold, the increase in its value isn't subject to taxation.

Instead of selling these assets to fund a lifestyle or ventures, individuals borrow against them. This borrowing is facilitated through securities-backed loans, where the appreciating asset serves as collateral. It's a clever maneuver: The loan provides liquidity without triggering a taxable event, as loans aren't considered income by the IRS. This means you can access the value of your investments to fund anything from business expansions to personal endeavors, all while your assets continue to appreciate. The interest paid on these loans may even be tax-deductible (depending on what you're borrowing for), further enhancing the strategy's allure. By using your assets as collateral, you effectively unlock their value without incurring immediate tax liabilities. This is what I did to buy 10 properties in 5 years by leveraging the appreciation in the value of our principal place of residence along with savings. When you use these funds to buy residential investment properties, it means the money I borrowed against our house plus the loan on the investment property was 100% tax deductible - win, win!

Upon one's passing, this strategy takes a final turn with the step-up in basis. When heirs inherit assets, the cost basis of these assets is adjusted to their current market value at the time of inheritance. This adjustment effectively wipes out any capital gains that accumulated during the original owner's lifetime, significantly reducing the tax burden for the heirs. For example, consider a piece of real estate purchased decades ago for $200,000 that has appreciated to $1 million. If the owner sells during their lifetime, they'd face capital gains tax on $800,000. However, if the property is inherited, the heir's taxable gain is based on the $1 million value, not the original purchase price, often resulting in little to no capital gains tax upon eventual sale. This aspect of the strategy highlights its effectiveness in preserving wealth across generations.

While the "Buy, Borrow, Die" approach offers numerous advantages, it's not without its risks and ethical considerations. Market volatility presents a significant challenge; the value of assets used as collateral can fluctuate, potentially leading to a margin call where the lender demands additional collateral or loan repayment. This risk necessitates careful asset selection and diligent market monitoring. What does this mean in plain English? If you are going to borrow against an asset class, a good one is residential or commercial real estate as, generally, these asset classes consistently go up in value. Borrowing against an asset class like shares or crypto is higher risk, and likely, if you did get lending, it would be less.

In this strategy, careful planning is paramount. Choosing assets wisely, starting early, and ensuring robust estate planning are crucial steps to maximizing benefits and mitigating risks. It's advisable to seek guidance from financial and tax professionals who can tailor the strategy to your unique circumstances and navigate the complexities involved. Understanding the nuances of leveraging assets without selling, capitalizing on loans, and the implications of inheritance can empower you to make informed decisions. By integrating these components thoughtfully, you can not only fortify your financial foundation but also pave the way for future generations to thrive.

3.2 Leveraging Tax Shelters for Savings

Picture tax shelters as protective umbrellas, allowing you to shield a portion of your income from the tax collector's reach, legally and effectively. These financial structures are designed to reduce your taxable income, providing a legitimate way to save money while aligning with your long-term financial strategy. One of the most recognized forms of tax shelter is the retirement account. Accounts such as 401(k)s and IRAs are popular tools that allow contributions to grow tax-deferred, meaning you won't pay taxes on your earnings until you withdraw the funds, typically in retirement when you may be in a lower tax bracket. This delay in taxation enables your investments to compound over time, significantly increasing their value. By prioritizing contributions to these accounts, you not only prepare for future needs but also enjoy immediate tax benefits.

Beyond retirement accounts, there are numerous tax shelters available to individuals, each offering unique advantages. Municipal bonds, for example, are an appealing option for those seeking tax-free income. These bonds, issued by local governments, provide interest payments that are often exempt from federal taxes and, in some cases, state and local taxes as well. This tax exemption can result in a higher effective yield compared to taxable bonds, making them a valuable addition to a diversified portfolio. Real estate investments also serve as robust tax shelters, offering depreciation deductions and the opportunity to defer capital gains taxes through tools like the 1031 Exchange. By investing in real estate, you can benefit from both the appreciation of property value and the reduction of taxable income.

Choosing the right tax shelter involves a thoughtful assessment of your individual financial situation. It's crucial to match the shelter to your financial goals, considering factors such as risk tolerance, investment horizon, and future income expectations. For instance, if your primary aim is to generate a steady, tax-free income, municipal bonds might be the ideal choice. Alternatively, if you're focused on long-term growth and are comfortable with the responsibilities of property management, real estate may offer the most significant benefits. The key is to align these shelters with your broader financial strategy, ensuring they complement your overall wealth-building objectives.

While the allure of tax shelters is undeniable, it's imperative to remain vigilant against the temptation of illegal or overly aggressive schemes. The line between legal tax avoidance and illegal tax evasion can sometimes blur, particularly when complex strategies are involved. Abusive tax shelters, often marketed as too-good-to-be-true solutions, promise substantial tax savings but can lead to significant legal repercussions. The IRS closely monitors such arrangements, and involvement in them can result in hefty fines, penalties, and even criminal charges. It's vital to stay informed and cautious, prioritizing transparency and compliance with tax laws. Consulting with a knowledgeable tax advisor can provide clarity and ensure that your tax minimization efforts remain within legal boundaries.

In exploring tax shelters, imagine them as tools in a well-stocked toolbox, each designed for a specific purpose and situation. By understanding how to utilize these tools, you create a framework for financial stability and growth. Consider reflecting on your current financial strategy. Are there opportunities to incorporate tax shelters that align with your goals? Engaging in this exploration can reveal new paths to financial efficiency, allowing you to retain more of your income to support the life you envision.

3.3 Maximizing Health Savings Account Benefits

Imagine a financial tool that not only helps you save for healthcare expenses but also offers a trifecta of tax advantages. Health Savings Accounts (HSAs) are exactly that—a versatile vehicle designed to provide significant tax benefits while supporting your health-related financial needs. When you contribute to an HSA, you do so with pre-tax dollars, which immediately reduces your taxable income for the year. This means you pay less in taxes upfront, effectively boosting your immediate savings. Moreover, any interest or investment earnings your HSA accumulates grow tax-free, further enhancing your financial position. Finally, when you withdraw funds from your HSA for qualified medical expenses, those withdrawals are also tax-free, adding a layer of financial efficiency that few other accounts can match.

Contributing to an HSA is straightforward, but maximizing its benefits requires mindful planning. Each year, the IRS sets contribution limits for HSAs—$3,650 for individuals and $7,300 for families in 2023, with an additional $1,000 catch-up contribution allowed for those over 55. Staying within these limits is crucial to avoid penalties. Contributions can be made directly or through payroll deductions, and they can be adjusted throughout the year to align with any changes in your financial or medical needs. When it comes to withdrawals, it's important to keep detailed records of all medical expenses to ensure compliance with HSA rules and avoid any potential tax complications. Notably, unlike some other medical savings plans, funds in an HSA roll over year after year, allowing for accumulation and growth without the pressure of a "use-it-or-lose-it" scenario.

So let's show this example. Consider you earn $63,650 per annum in your job. If you paid tax as normal with no deductions or credits, you would be taxed at the full $63,650. If you contribute the maximum $3,650 into an HSA Adjusted Gross Income (AGI) is now $60,000, which, depending on your state, means your net take-home pay increases from $58,038 to $58,491. So, by contributing money into an HSA, your take-home pay actually gets better, so the IRS rewards you for saving for your future. If it doesn't change your net pay position, why would you not make these contributions?

One of the most compelling aspects of HSAs is their potential to serve as long-term investment vehicles. Beyond covering immediate medical expenses, HSAs can be invested in mutual funds, stocks, or other securities, similar to a retirement account. This investment aspect transforms the HSA from a simple savings tool into a powerful component of your long-term financial strategy. Over time, the growth within an HSA can be substantial, particularly if you can afford to pay out-of-pocket for current medical expenses and allow your HSA funds to remain invested. This approach not only maximizes the account's growth potential but also aligns with retirement planning strategies, providing a tax-advantaged way to save for healthcare costs in your later years.

However, to fully benefit from an HSA, it's important to avoid common pitfalls. One frequent mistake is contributing beyond the annual limit, which can lead to penalties and excess contributions that must be withdrawn and reported as income. It's also crucial to use HSA funds exclusively for qualified medical expenses; non-qualified withdrawals are subject to taxes and a 20% penalty if you're under 65. Another oversight is neglecting to invest the funds within the HSA, which can result in missed opportunities for growth. To avoid these errors, regularly review your HSA contributions and expenses and consider consulting with a financial advisor to ensure optimal account management.

As you consider incorporating an HSA into your financial strategy, think about how it can complement your existing plans. Are there ways to adjust your contributions to maximize tax savings? How might investment options within an HSA align with your long-term goals? Exploring these questions can reveal new pathways to enhance your financial well-being, making the most of this versatile and tax-efficient tool.

3.4 The Power of Tax Deferral Tactics

Imagine having the ability to push today's tax burdens into the future, allowing your investments to flourish unencumbered. This is the magic of tax deferral, a strategy that can offer significant financial advantages by delaying the recognition of income. By postponing taxes, you grant your investments more time to grow, potentially resulting in a much larger nest egg by the time taxes are due. This approach leverages the time value of money, where dollars saved today can be worth more tomorrow due to compounding growth. Tax deferral doesn't eliminate your tax obligations, but it strategically delays them, providing more control over when taxes are paid, often at a time when your taxable income might be lower, such as in retirement.

One of the most common vehicles for tax deferral is the 401(k) plan. This employer-sponsored retirement account allows you to contribute pre-tax dollars, reducing your taxable income in the year of contribution. These contributions then grow tax-deferred until you begin withdrawals, ideally in retirement when your income—and thus your tax bracket—might be lower. Another tool is the deferred compensation plan, often available to high-income earners. It allows employees to defer a portion of their salary until a future date, again postponing tax liability until the funds are accessed. Both of these vehicles underscore the principle of tax deferral: paying taxes later, not now, and in doing so, potentially paying less overall.

Implementing tax deferral strategies effectively requires foresight and planning. Timing is crucial. Consider structuring your income to fall in years when you're in a lower tax bracket. For instance, if you foresee a year with reduced income—perhaps due to a sabbatical or a planned career change—you might choose to defer income to that year to minimize your tax hit. Similarly, taking advantage of market downturns to convert traditional retirement accounts to Roth accounts can be beneficial. This conversion involves paying taxes at the time of conversion, but it allows for future growth and withdrawals to be tax-free. It's a strategy that requires careful calculation to balance immediate tax costs with long-term benefits.

However, tax deferral isn't without its complexities and potential pitfalls. Required Minimum Distributions (RMDs) are a key consideration. Once you reach age 73, RMDs mandate that you begin withdrawing from your traditional retirement accounts, whether you need the money or not. These withdrawals are taxable, which can sometimes push you into a higher tax bracket. It's crucial to plan for RMDs well in advance, possibly by gradually converting some traditional accounts to Roth accounts before reaching the mandatory withdrawal age. This proactive approach can help manage your tax bracket and avoid unexpected tax liabilities. Be sure to seek advice from a tax professional well in advance.

Tax deferral offers a powerful way to manage when and how much you pay in taxes, but it requires careful planning and an understanding of the rules governing various deferral vehicles. It's about making informed decisions today to shape a more favorable financial future. As you navigate these strategies, consider how each element of tax deferral fits into your larger financial picture, ensuring that you maximize the benefits while staying mindful of potential challenges and obligations that may arise down the road.

3.5 Utilizing Charitable Contributions for Tax Benefits

Consider the impact of giving on both your heart and your wallet. Charitable donations not only support causes that resonate with your values but also offer a dual advantage by reducing your taxable income. When you donate to a qualified charity, the amount is deductible from your taxable income, which can lead to significant tax savings. This reduction means you owe less to the IRS, allowing you to redirect those funds to further philanthropic efforts or personal financial goals. By strategically incorporating charitable giving into your financial plan, you can make a meaningful difference in the world while also benefiting your bottom line.

However, to effectively claim these deductions, understanding the rules and limitations is crucial. The IRS sets specific guidelines on how much you can deduct, often based on a percentage of your adjusted gross income (AGI). Generally, you can deduct up to 60% of your AGI for cash contributions, though this limit may vary depending on the type of donation and the organization. It's vital to keep thorough records, including receipts and acknowledgment letters, to substantiate your claims. This diligence ensures that your contributions meet IRS requirements and that you maximize the available deductions. With the correct documentation, you can confidently include these deductions in your tax return, enhancing your financial flexibility.

For those looking to optimize their charitable impact while maximizing tax efficiency, advanced giving strategies can offer significant benefits. Donor-advised funds (DAFs) are one such tool, allowing you to donate cash or assets, receive an immediate tax deduction, and recommend grants to your preferred charities over time. This flexibility lets you plan your giving, making contributions in years when you seek additional deductions and distributing them when it aligns with your philanthropic goals. A case in point is the Thompson family, who used a donor-advised fund to manage their charitable donations. By contributing appreciated stock, they avoided capital gains tax and received a fair market value deduction, all while supporting their chosen causes with greater impact.

Another sophisticated strategy involves charitable remainder trusts (CRTs), which provide income for you or your beneficiaries and eventually benefit your selected charities. By transferring assets into a CRT, you not only receive an immediate tax deduction based on the trust's value but also enjoy potential income tax deferral on the trust's growth. This approach combines philanthropy with income planning, offering a way to maintain financial stability while committing to charitable work. These advanced strategies require careful planning and consultation with financial advisors to ensure they align with your broader financial objectives and comply with legal requirements.

A strategic approach to charitable giving aligns your philanthropic endeavors with your personal financial goals. Developing a giving plan can help clarify these goals, ensuring your donations not only reflect your values but also fit seamlessly into your overall financial picture. Start by identifying the causes that matter most to you, then determine how much of your income you wish to allocate. Consider the timing and method of your contributions, whether through direct donations, donor-advised funds, or charitable remainder trusts. This thoughtful planning ensures that your generosity is both impactful and tax-efficient.

Incorporating charitable contributions into your tax strategy offers a powerful way to support what you care about while managing your financial responsibilities. By understanding the rules and exploring advanced giving options, you can enhance the impact of your donations and optimize your tax situation. With a clear giving plan, you balance generosity with financial prudence, ensuring your contributions benefit both the causes you love and your own financial health.

As we wrap up this chapter on tax minimization strategies, remember that each tactic is a piece of the larger financial puzzle, working together to create a more secure and prosperous future. A lot of these strategies are complex and ways that people with large incomes can minimize their tax, but I thought I'd include it, as who knows, you might win the lottery and have a tax problem on your hands! Feel free to disregard it if it's not for you, but I thought it's better to know a little so it's on your radar as your income grows.

Don't move on to the next chapter without doing the following;

1. Do you have an asset that you can borrow against to release funds to buy another appreciating asset? Get advice on your wealth accumulation strategy from a CPA accountant
2. Do you have a retirement account set up? You should begin saving for your retirement as soon as you can, particularly if your company has an employer-match scheme. I have a whole other book on Retirement Planning Made Easy, but, needless to say, it's time to start investigating the options if you don't have one. Contact your HR department for further information
3. Do you have an HSA set up? Should you? The cost of healthcare in the US is crazy ridiculous, so you need to be putting money aside for this immediately. This is a no-brainer. Again contact your HR department for further information
4. Do you want to make charitable giving part of your tax strategy? Ensure your chosen charity can issue you a tax invoice and that the funds are transferred out of your account pre the 31st of December in the year you want to claim to enable it to be part of that year's tax return

Chapter 4

Navigating Complex Tax Scenarios

Picture yourself juggling multiple balls in the air, each representing a different source of income. This is the reality for many people today, where multiple income streams are not just a luxury but a necessity. Whether you're balancing a full-time job with a side hustle, earning rental income from a property, or diving into freelance work, the complexity of managing these diverse streams can quickly become overwhelming. Each one comes with its own set of tax implications, and without a clear strategy, you might find yourself entangled in a web of tax forms and obligations. The key to successfully navigating this landscape lies in understanding the nuances of each income type and how they interact with your overall tax picture.

When you receive income from a traditional employer, it's typically reported on a W-2 form. This form includes details on wages, salaries, and taxes withheld, making it relatively straightforward. However, things get more intricate when you add 1099 income into the mix. Unlike W-2 employees, 1099 workers, such as freelancers or contractors, don't have taxes withheld from their paychecks. This means you're responsible for estimating and paying your taxes quarterly, a task that can catch many off guard. It's crucial to accurately report both W-2 and 1099 income to avoid penalties and ensure compliance with tax regulations. Rental income adds another layer of complexity. If you own a rental property, you're required to report the income received from tenants, as well as any expenses incurred for maintenance, repairs, and mortgage interest. This information is typically filed using Schedule E, which details income and expenses related to rental properties. Understanding how to accurately report these figures is essential for optimizing your tax outcome and avoiding costly mistakes.

For those with side hustles, the tax landscape can become even murkier. Whether you're driving for a ride-share service, selling crafts online, or offering consulting services, each venture brings with it specific tax responsibilities. Income from side hustles is generally considered self-employment income, requiring you to report it on Schedule C. This form allows you to deduct business-related expenses, such as office supplies, advertising costs, and travel expenses, reducing your taxable income. However, you'll also need to pay self-employment taxes, which cover Social Security and Medicare contributions. Estimating quarterly tax payments becomes essential to avoid underpayment penalties, as the IRS expects taxes to be paid as income is earned, not just at the end of the year.

Effectively managing tax liabilities with multiple income streams requires a strategic approach. One strategy involves combining incomes for tax efficiency. By consolidating your income sources and calculating your overall tax bracket, you can identify opportunities to reduce your tax burden. This may involve adjusting your withholdings or making estimated payments to ensure you're not overpaying or underpaying taxes throughout the year. Additionally, keeping detailed records of all income and expenses is vital for accurate reporting. This documentation not only simplifies the filing process but also supports your claims in the event of an audit.

Navigating the complexities of multiple income streams is no small feat, but with the right tools and knowledge, you can master this aspect of tax planning. By understanding the requirements for reporting diverse income types and implementing strategies to optimize your tax outcome, you set the stage for financial success. Embrace the challenge and use it as an opportunity to enhance your financial literacy and gain greater control over your tax situation.

Exercise: Income Stream Analysis

Take a moment to list all your income sources, categorizing them as W-2, 1099, rental, or other. Note any associated expenses and consider how they impact your overall tax picture. Are there deductions or credits you're not currently utilizing? Use this exercise to identify areas for optimization and strategic planning.

4.1 Understanding Capital Gains Taxes

Understanding capital gains taxes is like learning the rules of a game where the stakes are your financial future. Capital gains occur when you sell an asset, such as stocks, bonds, or real estate, for more than you paid for it. These gains are categorized into short-term and long-term, each with distinct tax implications. Short-term capital gains come from assets held for a year or less and are taxed at your regular income tax rate, which can be quite high. On the other hand, long-term capital gains from assets held for more than a year benefit from lower tax rates—typically 0%, 15%, or 20%, depending on your income level. This distinction is crucial because it directly impacts how much you owe the IRS when you cash in on your investments.

Capital gains can substantially influence your overall tax liability, particularly if you experience significant gains in any given year. A substantial capital gain can push you into a higher tax bracket or increase your taxable income substantially, leading to a steeper tax bill. The tax rates on long-term capital gains are structured to encourage long-term investment, rewarding patience with lower taxes. For example, if you fall within certain income thresholds, you might pay a mere 0% on long-term gains, a benefit not available for short-term gains, which are taxed as ordinary income. Understanding these rates helps you strategize and potentially lower your tax obligations, keeping more of your profits in your pocket.

To manage and minimize capital gains taxes, strategic planning is essential. One effective strategy is tax-loss harvesting, which involves selling investments at a loss to offset gains from other investments. This method can reduce your taxable income and, consequently, your tax bill. It's an approach that not only manages tax liabilities but also allows for portfolio re-balancing, potentially improving overall investment performance. Another critical tactic is understanding the holding period for your assets. Holding investments for longer than a year before selling elevates them from short-term to long-term status, thus qualifying for the lower tax rate on gains. This timing can be a deciding factor in how much tax you ultimately pay. Keep good records so you know the purchase dates of your investments.

Strategic planning around capital gains also involves timing your asset sales to coincide with years of lower income, thus reducing the overall tax impact. For instance, if you anticipate a year with lower income due to a sabbatical or reduced work hours, it might be advantageous to sell some of your long-term investments during that time. This can ensure you're taxed at the lowest possible rate. Additionally, taking advantage of tax-advantaged accounts like IRAs or 401(k)s can defer taxes on gains until withdrawal, potentially during retirement when your income—and tax rate—might be lower. This forward-thinking approach allows you to manage your tax liability proactively.

The complexities of capital gains taxes underscore the importance of careful planning and informed decision-making. By understanding how different assets are taxed and employing strategies such as tax-loss harvesting, strategic timing of sales, and leveraging tax-advantaged accounts, you can optimize your tax outcomes. These strategies not only reduce your immediate tax burden but also contribute to your long-term financial health, enabling you to grow your wealth more effectively.

4.2 Tax Considerations for Freelancers and Gig Workers

As a freelancer or gig worker, your tax obligations differ significantly from those of traditional employees. Unlike a regular job where taxes are automatically withheld from your paycheck, you're responsible for calculating and paying them yourself. This includes self-employment taxes, which cover

Social Security and Medicare contributions that an employer would typically handle. The self-employment tax rate is 15.3% for most individuals, encompassing both the employee and employer portions of these contributions. Understanding and managing these obligations is crucial to avoid any end-of-year surprises. Additionally, you're required to make estimated tax payments quarterly. These payments are based on your expected income and help you stay current with your tax liabilities throughout the year, preventing the accumulation of a large tax bill at filing time.

Tracking your income and expenses accurately is vital for freelancers. With multiple clients and varied sources of income, maintaining precise financial records is essential. Consider using accounting software tailored to freelancers. These tools can automate the process of tracking income, categorizing expenses, and generating reports, making it easier to stay organized. They can also help you keep a clear record of invoices sent and payments received, ensuring that you don't overlook any taxable income. Regularly updating your records prevents the buildup of paperwork and ensures that you can access your financial data when tax season rolls around. This software can also help you file your quarterly taxes, telling you which fields you should enter on your quarterly tax return.

Freelancers have access to several deductions that can significantly reduce taxable income. One of the most common is the home office deduction. If you work from a dedicated space in your home, you can claim a portion of your rent or mortgage, utilities, and other related expenses. The IRS offers a simplified option for this deduction, allowing you to claim $5 per square foot of home office space, up to 300 square feet. Additionally, expenses related to equipment necessary for your work, such as computers and software, are deductible. If your work involves travel, you can also deduct associated costs, including airfare, lodging, and meals, provided they are directly related to your business activities. Even the cost of meals consumed during business meetings or while traveling for work can be partially deducted, offering further relief.

Managing cash flow is another critical aspect for freelancers. Setting aside a percentage of your income for taxes helps ensure that you have the funds available when estimated tax payments are due. A good rule of thumb is to reserve around 25-30% of your income for tax purposes. Ensure you are charging enough for your services to cover these costs, as otherwise, you're taking home less than you would have as a W2 employee. This approach ensures you're not caught off guard when it's time to make payments. You might also consider setting up a separate bank account specifically for tax savings, which can prevent the temptation to dip into these funds for other expenses. Regularly reviewing your cash flow and adjusting your savings as your income fluctuates can keep your finances stable and prepare you for any unforeseen changes in your tax situation.

Navigating the tax landscape as a freelancer requires diligence and foresight. By understanding your obligations and leveraging available deductions, you can manage your tax liabilities effectively. With the right tools and strategies, you can focus on what you do best—whether it's writing, designing, coding, or any other freelance work—while maintaining a solid financial footing.

4.3 Handling Stock Options and Equity Compensation

In the realm of employment benefits, stock options and equity compensation present unique opportunities and challenges for employees seeking to maximize their financial rewards. Understanding the different types of stock options available, such as Non-qualified Stock Options (NSOs) and Incentive Stock Options (ISOs), is crucial for managing the tax implications that accompany them. NSOs are the more common type and do not qualify for special tax treatment under the Internal Revenue Code. When you exercise NSOs, the difference between the stock's market price (the price on the day the stock is vested to you) and the exercise price (the price on the day the stock is given to you) is considered taxable income, subject to ordinary income tax rates. This income is typically reported on your W-2 form. ISOs, however, offer potential tax benefits. If you meet specific holding requirements (hold the shares for 12 months post the exercise date), the gain from exercising ISOs can be taxed at the more favorable long-term capital gains rate instead of ordinary income rates (if held for less than 12 months). Yet, the exercise of ISOs can trigger the Alternative Minimum Tax (AMT), a separate tax system designed to ensure that high earners pay a minimum amount of tax. The AMT can complicate matters, as it requires understanding both regular tax liabilities and AMT liabilities, making tax planning even more critical.

Exercising stock options can significantly impact your taxable income. For NSOs, the exercise itself creates taxable income, which may push you into a higher tax bracket. Planning the timing of your exercise is essential to manage your tax liability effectively. For instance, exercising options in a year when your income is lower can help reduce the overall tax burden. With ISOs, while exercising does not immediately create taxable income for regular tax purposes, it does affect your AMT calculation. If you hold the shares long enough to qualify for long-term capital gains treatment, you can benefit from lower tax rates on the sale. However, careful consideration of the AMT is necessary, as it can negate some of the tax advantages if not planned correctly.

To optimize the tax impact of stock options, strategic planning is key. Timing your exercises and sales can help control when and how much tax you pay. For example, if you anticipate an increase in income or a change in tax rates, exercising options before these events can lock in lower tax rates. The disadvantage of exercising options is that you have to fund the purchase of your exercised options when they vest. A lot of people are then keen to offset this financial outlay by selling them and recognizing the gain, but because you've held them for less than 12 months, this will be treated as income tax, whereas if you held them for longer than 12 months you would minimize tax via capital gains tax rules. Diversifying your stock portfolio is also a prudent strategy. Relying heavily on your employer's stock can be risky, both in terms of investment and tax liability. By diversifying, you reduce concentration risk and potentially manage tax impacts more effectively, as you can choose when to realize gains and losses across a broader portfolio.

Be mindful of common pitfalls when dealing with stock options. A frequent mistake is double counting income, which occurs when employees fail to adjust their cost basis after exercising options. This can lead to over-reporting income when the stock is eventually sold. What this means is you would have already paid tax on the difference between the exercise and market price. If you choose, then sell them later for a higher market price, the only gain you need to pay tax on is the difference between what you sell them at and the market price, not the exercise price, as you've already paid tax on this. Ensure that you account for the compensation income recognized at exercise when determining the basis of your stock. Additionally, misunderstanding the holding period requirements for ISOs can result in unexpected tax consequences if the stock is sold too soon, converting what could have been a capital gain into ordinary income. Careful record-keeping and consultation with tax professionals can help navigate these complexities.

Navigating the world of stock options and equity compensation requires a keen understanding of both the benefits and the tax implications. By strategically timing exercises and sales, diversifying your holdings, and avoiding common mistakes, you can maximize the financial rewards while minimizing tax liabilities. The landscape of equity compensation is nuanced, but with careful planning, it can be a valuable component of your overall financial strategy.

4.4 Real Estate Investments and Tax Implications

Owning real estate can be a lucrative venture, providing both income and potential tax benefits. One significant advantage is the ability to claim depreciation deductions. Depreciation allows you to reduce your taxable income by accounting for the wear and tear on your property over time. This deduction spreads the cost of the property over its useful life, typically 27.5 years for residential real estate. By reducing your taxable income, depreciation can significantly lower your tax liability each year. However, it's important to understand that the depreciation recapture tax will apply when you sell the property, adding back the depreciation deductions you've claimed. Another factor is the passive activity loss rules, which limit the ability to deduct losses from rental activities against other types of income. These rules can complicate tax planning, especially if you're not actively involved in the property's management. However, meeting the criteria of a real estate professional can allow you to deduct these losses more freely, offering additional flexibility. As your accountant how you would qualify to be a real estate professional.

Reporting rental income and expenses accurately is crucial for real estate investors. The IRS requires you to report all rental income you receive, including any advance rent or security deposits used as rent. Deductions for expenses related to maintaining and operating the property can significantly reduce your taxable income. Common deductions include mortgage interest, property tax, operating expenses, and repairs. To report these figures, you'll use Schedule E, which details supplemental income and loss. This form requires a comprehensive record of all income and expenses associated with your rental properties, emphasizing the importance of meticulous record-keeping. By maintaining clear and detailed records, you ensure that you can support your claims in the event of an audit and optimize your tax outcome.

Selling real estate introduces another layer of tax considerations. If your property has appreciated in value, you'll face capital gains taxes on the profit. However, the IRS offers tools to defer these taxes, such as the 1031 exchange. This provision allows you to defer paying capital gains taxes by reinvesting the proceeds from a sale into another similar property. To qualify, you must identify the replacement property within 45 days and complete the purchase within 180 days. This strategy can be a powerful tool for investors looking to grow their real estate portfolios without the immediate tax burden. Keep in mind that while 1031 exchanges defer taxes, they don't eliminate them, and careful planning is essential to maximize their benefits.

Real estate investing offers a unique blend of income opportunities and tax benefits, but it requires careful planning and an understanding of the tax code. Before you purchase a property, you should speak to a tax accountant to ensure you have the correct structure in place to buy the property, whether that's in your personal name, an LLC, or a trust. Given how litigious the US has become, it's important to protect your wealth from being lost. Each decision, from purchasing to selling, carries tax implications that can affect your overall financial strategy. By leveraging the available tools and strategies, you can optimize your tax situation and make the most of your real estate investments.

4.5 Managing Taxes for Small Business Owners

Running a small business is a bit like juggling. You have multiple responsibilities, and taxes are a big part of that. As a business owner, you're responsible for paying various taxes. Payroll taxes are one of the big ones. These are amounts you withhold from employee wages to cover Social Security and Medicare, along with your employer contributions. Business income taxes are another major responsibility. Depending on your business structure, these could be personal or corporate taxes. Staying on top of these keeps your business running smoothly and legally. Understanding these taxes and how they affect your business is crucial for success.

Choosing the right business structure is a foundational decision that impacts your taxes. A sole proprietorship is the simplest structure, where the income is reported on your personal tax return, making it straightforward but potentially taxing at higher personal rates. An LLC, or Limited Liability Company, offers liability protection and tax flexibility, allowing you to choose how you want the business to be taxed, often as a sole proprietor or partnership. Then, there's an S-corporation. It combines the benefits of incorporation with the tax advantages of a partnership. S-corp owners can draw a salary and take profits as dividends, potentially reducing self-employment taxes. Each structure has its benefits and drawbacks, and understanding these can help you make the best choice for your business.

Good bookkeeping is the backbone of effective tax management. Accurate record-keeping not only helps you track income and expenses but also simplifies tax preparation and filing. Implementing accounting software is a practical step toward achieving this. Software like QuickBooks or Xero can automate many tasks, such as invoicing, expense tracking, and financial reporting. This automation reduces errors and frees up time for more strategic business activities. Regularly updating your records ensures that you have a clear financial picture, which is essential for making informed decisions and staying compliant with tax regulations.

Tax planning isn't just for big corporations. Small businesses can also benefit from strategic tax planning to minimize liabilities. One effective strategy is utilizing Section 179 expensing, which allows you to deduct the full purchase price of qualifying equipment or software purchased or financed during the tax year. This can lead to significant tax savings and improve cash flow. Additionally, setting up retirement plans for yourself and your employees can offer tax benefits. Contributions to SEP IRAs or SIMPLE IRAs are tax-deductible, reducing taxable income while providing valuable retirement savings for you and your team. These strategies not only reduce your tax burden but also support the long-term financial health of your business.

By understanding your tax obligations, selecting an appropriate business structure, maintaining accurate records, and employing strategic tax planning, you can manage your business taxes effectively. These practices not only ensure compliance but also enhance financial stability, allowing you to focus on growing your business. As we wrap up this chapter, remember that tax management is an integral part of running a successful business, and mastering it can provide a solid foundation for sustained growth and prosperity.

Don't move on to the next chapter without doing the following;

1. List all your income sources and determine whether you are claiming all the deductions you possibly can against that income
2. If you are self-employed, set up reminders for quarterly filing dates so you don't forget. There's an online tax calendar in the references section of the book
3. Do you have stock options as part of your package? Understand your vesting schedule by planning when they vest and potentially planning to offset this income against a potential loss in your portfolio or strategically

planning your tax for that year

4. Have you chosen accounting software to run your business? Have a look at the tutorials of Xero or QuickBooks

Chapter 5

Real-Life Case Studies and Stories

Picture a bustling kitchen where a couple hurriedly prepares for a dinner party. The aroma of spices fills the air, mirroring the blend of anticipation and anxiety they feel about their upcoming tax season. Meet Lisa and Mark, a couple whose dual incomes placed them in a high tax bracket, causing their financial goals to simmer on the back burner. Like many, they felt the frustration of watching their hard-earned money dissipate through taxes, leaving them with less to invest in their future dreams. Determined to change their financial trajectory, they embarked on a quest to explore legal strategies that could alleviate their tax burdens and allow them to savor the fruits of their labor.

Lisa and Mark's primary challenge was their combined income, which nudged them into a higher tax bracket. The prospect of maximizing their earnings while minimizing taxes seemed daunting, yet they were resolute in their mission. They began by scrutinizing their financial landscape, identifying areas ripe for strategic planning. The first step was maximizing their retirement contributions. By channeling more funds into their 401(k)s and IRAs, they effectively reduced their taxable income, gaining immediate tax benefits while securing their future. This move not only lowered their current tax bill but also fortified their retirement nest egg, laying the groundwork for long-term financial security.

In addition to retirement contributions, Lisa and Mark explored the potential of tax credits for energy-efficient home improvements. They realized that upgrading their home with energy-efficient windows, insulation, and appliances could yield substantial tax credits. These improvements aligned with their values of sustainability, offering the dual benefit of reducing their carbon footprint and their tax liability. By claiming these credits, they further decreased their taxable income, effectively saving thousands of dollars. This approach demonstrated the power of aligning personal values with financial strategy, transforming their home into both an eco-friendly haven and a financial asset.

The tangible impact of these strategies was profound. Lisa and Mark successfully reduced their taxable income by $10,000, a significant achievement that resonated throughout their financial planning. With the money saved on taxes, they were able to reinvest in their future, contributing more to their children's education fund and exploring new investment opportunities. The financial relief also afforded them greater peace of mind, knowing that they were maximizing their resources and aligning their finances with their goals.

Reflecting on their journey, Lisa and Mark gleaned several key insights. They discovered the importance of proactive tax planning—an ongoing process rather than a last-minute rush. By engaging with their finances throughout the year, they were able to adjust their strategies in real time, optimizing their tax outcomes and ensuring alignment with their broader financial goals. They also recognized the value of professional guidance, consulting with tax advisors who provided expertise and insights that illuminated their path. This collaboration empowered them to navigate the complexities of the tax code with confidence, unlocking opportunities they might have otherwise overlooked.

Their experience underscores the transformative potential of tax literacy and strategic planning. By approaching their taxes with intention and foresight, Lisa and Mark not only eased their immediate tax burden but also set the stage for sustained financial growth. Their journey serves as a reminder that with the right tools and guidance, you too, can turn the tide on tax challenges, channeling savings into the aspirations that matter most to you.

Exercise: Reflecting on Your Tax Strategy

Take a moment to evaluate your current tax strategy. Are there opportunities to maximize retirement contributions or explore tax credits for home improvements? Consider your goals and values, and identify areas where strategic planning could enhance your financial position. Set aside time to research or consult with a professional, and take proactive steps to align your tax planning with your broader financial objectives.

5.1 The Freelancer's Guide to Avoiding Common Tax Pitfalls

Imagine stepping into the shoes of a freelancer, where freedom and flexibility come hand in hand with uncertainty. Meet Sam, a graphic designer who embraced the independent lifestyle, thriving on the creative freedom it allowed. However, Sam quickly discovered that managing an inconsistent income stream was like walking a financial tightrope. Without the safety net of a steady paycheck, budgeting became a complex dance of balancing client payments and personal expenses. The fluctuating nature of freelance work made it difficult to predict annual earnings, adding layers of complexity to tax obligations. Sam faced the challenge of anticipating tax liabilities, a task that often felt as volatile as his income.

One of the first hurdles Sam encountered was underestimating quarterly tax payments. Like many freelancers, he learned the hard way that failing to accurately estimate taxes throughout the year could result in a hefty year-end bill. Sam initially assumed that paying taxes was a once-a-year task, only to be caught off guard by penalties for underpayment. To overcome this, he began setting aside a fixed percentage of each payment received, creating a dedicated tax fund. This method ensured that he had sufficient funds when quarterly payments were due, reducing stress and avoiding penalties. This simple change in approach transformed his tax planning from a reactive scramble to a proactive routine.

Another significant pitfall was the misclassification of business expenses. In the early days of freelancing, Sam struggled to distinguish between personal and business expenses, often mixing them in a single account. This lack of clarity led to missed deductions and a higher taxable income than necessary. To address this, Sam implemented a dedicated business account, a decision that streamlined his record-keeping and clarified his financial picture. By separating his finances, Sam could accurately track business-related expenses such as software subscriptions, travel costs, and office supplies. This clear delineation allowed him to claim legitimate deductions confidently, lowering his tax burden and improving financial transparency.

Over time, Sam's approach to taxes evolved significantly. He began to view tax planning as an integral part of his business strategy rather than a dreaded chore. By incorporating tools like accounting software to track expenses and income, Sam gained better insights into his financial health. This newfound clarity enabled him to forecast his earnings more accurately, leading to more precise tax estimates. With a structured system in place, Sam felt empowered to focus on growing his business without the constant worry of unexpected tax liabilities lurking around the corner.

For freelancers like Sam, keeping detailed records of all transactions is not just a recommendation—it's a necessity. Accurate documentation serves as both a shield and a sword, protecting against audits and enhancing the ability to maximize deductions. Sam's experience highlights the importance of maintaining meticulous records, from saving receipts to logging mileage for client visits. By doing so, he ensured that every legitimate expense was accounted for, maximizing his deductions and minimizing his tax liability. This practice also provided peace of mind, knowing that his financial house was in order should the IRS come knocking.

Freelancers navigating the complexities of taxes can glean valuable lessons from Sam's journey. Establishing a dedicated business account to separate personal and professional finances is a game-changer. It not only simplifies tax preparation but also enhances financial clarity. Embracing the habit of setting aside a portion of each payment for taxes prevents the shock of year-end tax bills, transforming tax season from a source of anxiety to a manageable aspect of business operations. Adopting these strategies can lead to a more stable financial footing, allowing freelancers to thrive in their creative pursuits without being bogged down by tax woes.

5.2 A Small Business Turnaround Through Smart Tax Planning

Imagine a bustling neighborhood cafe, once the heart of its community, now struggling to keep its doors open. The owner, Sarah, faced mounting challenges as the business's cash flow issues began to choke daily operations. Bills piled up faster than coffee orders, and Sarah realized she needed to find a way to stabilize her finances. The cafe's expenses consistently outpaced its income, creating a cycle of financial strain that threatened its survival. Sarah knew she needed a strategic approach to revitalize her business and sought the guidance of a trusted financial advisor who could offer a fresh perspective on her tax strategy.

One of the first steps in the cafe's turnaround was restructuring the business entity. Initially operating as a sole proprietorship, Sarah's advisor suggested transitioning to an S-Corporation, a move that promised significant tax efficiency. This change allowed Sarah to separate her personal and business finances more effectively. By allocating a reasonable salary for herself and treating additional profits as dividends, she minimized self-employment taxes, creating a clearer financial picture. This restructuring reduced her tax liability and improved her ability to reinvest back into the cafe, addressing the cash flow issues that had been a persistent thorn in her side.

In addition to restructuring, Sarah's advisor introduced her to small business tax credits that she had previously overlooked. One such credit was the Employee Retention Credit, which provided a substantial offset against payroll taxes. This credit, designed to encourage businesses to keep employees on the payroll during challenging times, became a lifeline for Sarah's cafe. By leveraging this credit, Sarah not only kept her staff employed but also freed up cash reserves that were critical for operational stability. The newfound financial flexibility allowed her to explore marketing initiatives and menu innovations, attracting more customers and boosting revenue.

The strategic changes implemented by Sarah and her advisor yielded impressive results. The cafe's annual tax liability saw a significant reduction, providing immediate financial relief. This reduction directly translated into improved cash reserves, enabling Sarah to reinvest in her business with confidence. She upgraded outdated equipment, enhancing operational efficiency and customer satisfaction. The positive cash flow also allowed her to weather unexpected challenges, such as equipment breakdowns, without jeopardizing the cafe's financial health. The renewed stability not only preserved the cafe's place in the community but also set the stage for long-term growth and success.

Sarah's experience offers valuable insights for small business owners facing similar challenges. Regular financial reviews became a cornerstone of her strategy, allowing her to adapt quickly to changing circumstances. By keeping a close eye on her finances, she could identify potential issues before they escalated, enabling her to make informed decisions and capitalize on opportunities. The lessons learned from Sarah's turnaround highlight the importance of proactive tax planning as an integral part of business strategy. By exploring restructuring options and leveraging available credits, small business owners can unlock financial opportunities that support both immediate needs and future aspirations.

5.3 Real Estate Investor Success Stories

Meet Alex and Jamie, two real estate investors who saw potential not just in bricks and mortar but in the long-term appreciation of property values. Their motivations were clear: to build a diversified portfolio that could withstand market fluctuations and generate consistent returns. They focused on properties in burgeoning neighborhoods, areas where growth potential was high and competition was low. This strategic location selection was driven by extensive market research and a keen eye for emerging trends, ensuring that each investment was poised for appreciation over time.

To enhance their investment profitability, Alex and Jamie employed an array of sophisticated tax strategies. A cornerstone of their approach was the use of 1031 exchanges, a powerful tool that allowed them to defer capital gains taxes by reinvesting proceeds from property sales into new, "like-kind" properties. This strategy not only postponed tax liabilities but also enabled them to continually upgrade their portfolio, trading up for properties with greater value and potential. Each transaction was meticulously planned to align with their long-term goals, ensuring that their portfolio was not only expanding but also becoming more robust and resilient.

The tangible results of Alex and Jamie's strategic planning were impressive. Within five years, they had successfully doubled their property portfolio, an achievement that spoke volumes about their ability to navigate the real estate market with precision and foresight. The increased scale of their investments provided enhanced cash flow, allowing them to capitalize on additional opportunities and reinvest in further growth. Their success was not just measured in the number of properties owned but in the increased equity and financial security they had built. Each property served as a stepping stone, contributing to a financial foundation that promised stability and prosperity.

For aspiring real estate investors, Alex and Jamie's story offers invaluable lessons and best practices. Strategic location selection emerged as a critical factor in their success. By choosing properties in areas with high growth potential, they maximized appreciation and ensured a steady stream of rental income. This focus on location was complemented by a disciplined approach to market research, allowing them to identify opportunities before they became mainstream. Additionally, their commitment to leveraging tax strategies, such as 1031 exchanges, underscored the importance of understanding and utilizing available resources to enhance investment outcomes.

As you consider your own path in real estate investing, take a page from Alex and Jamie's playbook. Prioritize strategic location selection, focusing on areas with untapped potential and favorable growth prospects. Explore tax strategies that align with your investment objectives, and be proactive in seeking opportunities to defer taxes and reinvest in your portfolio. Real estate investing is not just about acquiring properties; it's about building a sustainable financial future through informed decisions and strategic planning. By approaching each investment with a clear vision and a calculated strategy, you can emulate the success of seasoned investors and achieve your financial goals.

5.4 The Side Hustler's Tax Journey

Balancing the demands of a full-time job while nurturing a blossoming side hustle requires a unique blend of dedication and resilience. Meet Olivia, a marketing manager by day and an artisan jewelry maker by night. Like many, her pursuit of an additional income stream stemmed from a desire to monetize her passion while bolstering her financial security. Her initial foray into the world of side hustling was driven by creativity and the allure of extra earnings, yet it quickly became apparent that juggling multiple income sources came with its own set of challenges. The complexities of managing her time, alongside the administrative burdens of her side business, became apparent as she navigated tax obligations and financial management.

The tax implications of operating a side hustle like Olivia's are multifaceted. Unlike her regular salary, her side income didn't include automatic tax withholdings, which meant she needed to be proactive in setting aside funds for tax purposes. Olivia learned that tracking her earnings meticulously was crucial to avoid surprises come tax season. Deducting business expenses became a vital strategy in managing her tax liability. Every purchase related to her jewelry business, from raw materials to marketing costs, was a potential deduction. By diligently keeping receipts and records, she could reduce her taxable income, ensuring she wasn't paying more than necessary to the IRS. This proactive approach not only helped Olivia manage her tax responsibilities but also provided a clearer picture of her business's profitability.

The financial benefits of Olivia's side hustle were significant, yet not without their challenges. Through disciplined expense management, she was able to increase her annual savings—an accomplishment that allowed her to reinvest in her business and explore new marketing avenues. However, the financial juggling act required constant vigilance. Balancing her primary job with her entrepreneurial venture meant that time was often stretched thin. The administrative tasks of bookkeeping and tax planning sometimes felt overwhelming, but the rewards of additional income and personal fulfillment were undeniable. Olivia's journey reflects the delicate balance many face when seeking to turn a passion into a profitable venture.

For those navigating similar paths, Olivia's experience offers practical insights. One of the most effective strategies she employed was setting aside a portion of her side income specifically for taxes. By earmarking funds for her quarterly tax payments, Olivia avoided the stress of a large year-end tax bill and ensured compliance with her tax obligations. This practice of financial foresight became a cornerstone of her business strategy, providing peace of mind and allowing her to focus on growth. Additionally, she found value in using digital tools to streamline her financial tracking. Apps designed for small business accounting, like Xero or QuickBooks, helped her maintain organized records, making tax time less daunting and more efficient.

The journey of balancing a full-time career with a side hustle requires a thoughtful approach to tax management. By understanding the tax implications and strategically planning expenses, those like Olivia can not only meet their obligations but also thrive financially. Her story serves as a reminder that with careful planning and dedication, the pursuit of additional income can lead to both personal satisfaction and financial success.

5.5 Lessons from High-Net-Worth Individuals

Imagine a world where every financial decision is meticulously calculated, aiming to keep wealth secure while minimizing tax burdens. High-net-worth individuals (HNWIs) often operate in this realm, employing sophisticated tax strategies that serve as a masterclass in financial acumen. One of their key tools is a trust, a legal arrangement that allows them to manage assets and preserve wealth across generations. Trusts provide a shield against hefty estate taxes, offering a way to transfer wealth while maintaining control over the distribution. For example, a family trust can be structured to ensure that assets are not only protected from creditors but also passed down to heirs with reduced tax liabilities, thus preserving the family's wealth for future generations.

Personalized tax planning is another cornerstone of the HNWI approach. Unlike a one-size-fits-all solution, personalized strategies take into account the unique financial situation and goals of the individual. Many HNWIs employ family office services, which act as a hub for managing their financial affairs. These services coordinate everything from investment management to tax strategy, ensuring a cohesive approach that aligns with their broader financial objectives. By tailoring strategies to their specific needs, they can optimize tax efficiency while pursuing personal and professional goals. This level of customization is key to maximizing benefits and minimizing risks, allowing them to navigate the complexities of the tax landscape with precision.

When it comes to managing complex tax scenarios, professional advisors play a pivotal role. HNWIs often rely on a team of experts, including tax attorneys and accountants, who bring a wealth of knowledge and experience to the table. These advisors collaborate to create and implement strategies that are both innovative and compliant with current tax laws. For instance, a tax attorney might work alongside an accountant to structure a business sale in a way that minimizes capital gains tax, ensuring that the transaction aligns with the individual's long-term financial plan. This collaborative approach not only enhances tax efficiency but also provides peace of mind, knowing that every decision is backed by expert advice.

The lessons from HNWIs extend beyond the wealthy, offering valuable insights for all taxpayers. One such insight is the power of strategic philanthropy for tax relief. By incorporating charitable giving into their financial plans, HNWIs can reduce their taxable income while supporting causes they care about. This approach not only yields tax benefits but also allows them to make a positive impact on society. Strategic philanthropy involves carefully selecting charities and timing donations to maximize tax deductions, a practice that can be adopted by anyone looking to align their financial goals with their values. Whether you're donating to a local charity or setting up a donor-advised fund, giving back can be both financially rewarding and personally fulfilling.

In exploring these sophisticated strategies, the underlying theme is clear: informed, strategic planning is the key to financial success. Tailored tax strategies, the use of professional advisors, and a commitment to philanthropy are not just the domain of the wealthy—they are principles that can guide anyone toward better financial health. By adopting these practices, you can take control of your tax situation, make informed decisions, and work toward a future of financial stability and growth. As we move forward, consider how these lessons can apply to your own financial journey, setting the stage for the next chapter of your financial life, where you will continue to build on these foundations.

Don't move on to the next chapter without doing the following;

1. Have you evaluated your tax position? Are there ways you could be paying less tax while saving for retirement or claiming additional tax deductions? If needed, book an appointment with a tax advisor
2. Are there any of the examples that resonated with you? Do you need to set up a separate bank account and set aside taxes? Do that now before moving on

Chapter 6

Overcoming Tax Challenges and Fears

Imagine you're at a dinner party, and the conversation shifts to taxes. Suddenly, someone mentions the dreaded word: "audit." The room falls silent, and you can almost feel the collective tension as if an IRS agent might burst through the door at any moment. While the fear of an audit is common, the reality is far less dramatic than our imaginations often suggest. Understanding the true nature of IRS audits can transform this fear into a manageable aspect of tax planning.

6.1 Conquering the Fear of IRS Audits

Let's start with some numbers that might put your mind at ease. According to the IRS's 2023 Data Book, only about 0.44% of individual tax returns were audited in the fiscal year 2023. This figure means that less than one-half of one percent of all taxpayers were subject to an audit. The likelihood of being audited varies based on income levels and the complexity of your tax situation. For instance, individuals earning less than $400,000 annually saw no increase in audit rates, whereas those with higher incomes or more complex returns, such as those involving international activities or large deductions, faced a slightly greater risk.

Understanding what an audit entails can help reduce anxiety. The IRS typically initiates contact through a letter, not by phone or in person, detailing what they need to review. An audit might be conducted by mail or in person, depending on the complexity of the issues. Commonly requested documents include income statements, such as W-2s or 1099s, receipts for deductions, and other records verifying the information on your return. The process is systematic, and taxpayers have the opportunity to provide additional documentation or clarify any discrepancies. Auditors are not out to get you; they are simply performing their duties to ensure tax compliance.

Reducing the likelihood of an audit involves proactive measures. Accurate and honest reporting is crucial. Avoid red flags, such as claiming excessive deductions that are disproportionate to your income. For example, if your reported charitable contributions are significantly higher than average for your income bracket, it might catch the IRS's eye. Additionally, ensure that all reported figures match your documentation. Discrepancies between your W-2 or 1099 forms and your tax return can trigger further scrutiny. Consistently maintaining accuracy in your tax filings is one of the best defenses against an audit.

Preparation is key if you ever receive an audit notice. Organize your financial records, ensuring that all relevant documents are easily accessible. This includes income statements, receipts, and any correspondence with the IRS. Consider seeking professional representation if the audit involves complex issues or if you feel overwhelmed. A tax professional can guide you through the process, ensuring that your rights are protected and your case is presented effectively. Their expertise can be invaluable in navigating the nuances of tax law.

Exercise: Audit Readiness Checklist

Create a checklist of essential documents you would need in case of an audit. Start with income statements like W-2s and 1099s, then list deductions you claimed, such as mortgage interest or charitable contributions. Keep this checklist updated annually, and ensure all documents are organized and stored securely. This preparation can provide peace of mind, knowing you're ready should an audit ever arise.

By embracing a proactive approach and understanding the audit process, you can alleviate much of the fear associated with it. Taking steps to ensure accuracy, understanding how audits work, and knowing how to prepare in advance are powerful tools to manage and overcome the anxiety surrounding IRS audits.

6.2 Dispelling Myths About Tax Filing Complexity

Picture this: It's tax season, and the thought of filing your taxes looms over you like an insurmountable peak. You might believe that only seasoned professionals can navigate the complexities of tax returns, but this myth is more daunting than the reality. The notion that tax filing is reserved solely for experts has persisted for too long, leading many to avoid taking the reins of their financial responsibilities. While tax laws can be intricate, the process of filing your taxes is not as formidable as it seems. Many people successfully file their own taxes every year, armed with the right information and tools.

Breaking down tax filing into manageable steps can demystify the process. First, gather all necessary documents: W-2s from employers, 1099s for freelance income, receipts for deductible expenses, and any other relevant financial records. Having these documents organized and at hand streamlines your preparation. Set up a folder at the beginning of the year and put everything into it throughout the year. There's also a free spreadsheet you can use in the references section: Tax Expense Spreadsheet: Top 5 free templates. Next, select the appropriate tax forms. For most individuals, Form 1040 is the standard choice, but depending on your situation, you might need additional schedules for self-employment income or itemized deductions. Once your documents are in order, you can begin filling out the forms with your information, ensuring accuracy in every detail. Double-check your entries to prevent errors that could lead to complications later. Finally, submit your completed return, either electronically or by mail.

Resources abound for those who wish to file their taxes independently. The IRS offers Free File, a program providing guided tax preparation software for taxpayers with an Adjusted Gross Income (AGI) of $84,000 or less. Just Google IRS FreeFile, or there's a link for this in the references section. This program includes step-by-step assistance, helping you navigate your return with confidence. Many private companies also offer free or low-cost software solutions designed to simplify tax filing, like Cash App Taxes or TaxSlayer. These tools often include features that calculate deductions and credits, reducing the risk of human error. Additionally, the IRS website hosts a wealth of resources, from FAQs to detailed guides, all aimed at supporting taxpayers in understanding and managing their obligations. With these resources, even complex tax situations can be broken down into understandable parts.

Adopting a positive mindset toward tax filing can transform it from an annual chore into an empowering financial exercise. Engaging with your taxes directly enhances your financial literacy, granting you insight into your income, expenses, and potential savings. This understanding can help you make informed decisions throughout the year, from adjusting withholdings to planning deductions. Managing your taxes actively also fosters a sense of control over your financial life as you become more aware of how your financial choices impact your tax situation. Embrace this opportunity to learn and grow, turning tax season into a time for reflection and financial planning.

6.3 Avoiding the Pitfalls of Repetitive Content

As you navigate the world of tax information, you may notice that certain themes seem to echo repeatedly across different sources. This repetition can make it difficult to discern new insights from the same old advice. Whether it's the constant emphasis on saving receipts or the familiar refrain about retirement savings, repetitive content can feel like you're reading the same advice over and over. While some repetition serves to reinforce important principles, excessive redundancy can clutter your understanding and leave you feeling stuck in a loop. The challenge lies in differentiating between genuinely valuable information and content that merely treads old ground.

To cut through the noise, consider adopting a strategy where you cross-reference multiple sources. This method allows you to gain a broader perspective and verify the accuracy of the information you encounter. If several reputable sources agree on a point, you're likely on solid ground. However, if you notice discrepancies, it's an opportunity to dig deeper and understand why. This approach not only helps in identifying unique insights but also equips you with a more well-rounded understanding of the topic. It's equally helpful in spotting when different authors are just repeating the same advice without offering anything new.

Seeking diverse perspectives is another powerful tool in your arsenal. Tax advice doesn't just come in the form of books and articles. Podcasts and webinars offer fresh insights and often feature industry experts who provide real-time updates on changes and strategies. These formats can introduce you to innovative ideas and emerging trends that might not yet be widely covered in written literature. Engaging in tax forums and communities can also be enlightening. These platforms allow you to pose questions, share experiences, and learn from others who are navigating similar financial landscapes. They can be invaluable for gaining practical advice and alternative viewpoints that you might not encounter elsewhere. I know most of you won't be as dorky as I am and enjoy these things (!!), but it's always good to keep yourself informed, even if just subscribing to a newsletter you read once a month.

Critical thinking is your ally when it comes to evaluating tax information. Not every piece of advice you come across will be relevant or accurate. When you encounter a claim, consider its source. Is it coming from a reputable expert or a verified publication? Verifying information with official sources, such as the IRS website or well-established financial institutions, can safeguard against misinformation. Look for data and examples that support claims; well-substantiated advice often holds more weight. By honing your analytical skills, you can sift through the abundance of information available and focus on what's truly useful for your situation.

Resource List: Diverse Tax Perspectives

- Podcasts: "The Money Guy Show," "ChooseFI," and "Smart Passive Income"
- Webinars: Check platforms like Eventbrite and industry websites for upcoming tax-related webinars
- Forums: Reddit's r/tax and Bogleheads.org provide community-driven discussion and advice

Navigating tax literature effectively is about more than just consuming information. It's about actively engaging with content, challenging assumptions, and seeking out new ideas that resonate with your specific financial goals. By applying these strategies, you can navigate the sea of tax advice with confidence, armed with knowledge that is both relevant and valuable to your unique situation.

6.4 Understanding the Impact of Tax Law Changes

Tax laws are like the ever-shifting sands of a beach. They change with the tides of economic policy and government priorities. Staying informed about these changes is not just beneficial; it's crucial for effective tax planning. As laws evolve, so do the rules about deductions and credits, which can directly impact your tax responsibilities and opportunities. For instance, a change in the standard deduction can significantly alter the decision-making process about whether to itemize deductions. If the standard home office deduction increases, as it did in recent years, fewer taxpayers might find it beneficial to itemize, simplifying their filing process. This can lead to more straightforward tax returns but might also mean missing out on certain itemized deductions if they don't exceed the new standard amount. Understanding how these shifts affect you ensures that you make informed decisions that optimize your tax situation.

Recent tax law updates have brought several notable changes that could influence your tax planning. For example, the standard deduction amounts have been adjusted with increases designed to reflect inflation. These adjustments can mean a lower tax bill for many, as the amount of income not subject to tax is higher. Moreover, significant changes to the child tax credit have expanded eligibility and increased the credit's value, offering financial relief to more families. This update means that more parents can benefit from a reduced tax liability and, in some cases, receive a larger refund. Such changes highlight the importance of keeping abreast of current legislation, as they can have immediate and tangible effects on your finances.

Adapting to new tax laws requires a proactive approach. One of the first steps is revisiting your withholding allowances. Changes in tax laws might mean you're over-withholding or under-withholding based on outdated information. Adjusting your withholdings can ensure that you're not giving the government an interest-free loan of your money throughout the year or facing a large tax bill come April. It's a simple yet effective way to manage your cash flow in response to legislative changes. Additionally, reviewing your financial plan annually or when major tax law changes occur can help you incorporate new strategies that align with the current tax landscape. This might involve re-evaluating your retirement savings strategy or taking advantage of new credits that were previously unavailable to you.

To stay updated on tax law changes, consider tapping into reliable sources that provide timely and accurate information. Subscribing to IRS newsletters is a direct way to receive updates straight from the source. These newsletters often include information about upcoming changes, deadlines, and tips for taxpayers. Following reputable tax law blogs can also provide insights and analyses that help clarify complex legislative updates. These platforms often break down the implications of changes in a more digestible format, making it easier to understand how they affect you personally. By incorporating these resources into your routine, you can ensure that you're always in the loop, able to adapt your tax strategy proactively rather than reactively.

6.5 Accessing Personalized Tax Advice

Imagine walking into a tailor's shop, seeking a suit that fits you perfectly. Just as a bespoke suit is crafted to fit your unique body shape, personalized tax advice is tailored to fit the intricacies of your financial situation. Generic tax advice often fails to address the specific circumstances that make your financial landscape unique. From family dynamics and income sources to investment portfolios, each element requires a nuanced approach. Tailored guidance considers these complexities, offering strategies that align with your individual goals and challenges. This personalized approach ensures that you're not just following a one-size-fits-all plan but rather one that optimizes your financial health and tax efficiency.

The benefits of consulting a tax professional are manifold. When you enlist the help of an expert, you gain access to a wealth of knowledge, especially in complex tax scenarios. Professionals have the insight to navigate intricate tax codes and regulations, identifying opportunities for deductions and credits that you might overlook. This expertise translates into potential savings and accurate filings. Moreover, having a professional handle your taxes can provide peace of mind. Knowing that your return is prepared accurately and in compliance with current laws minimizes anxiety and reduces the risk of errors that could lead to audits or penalties. This assurance allows you to focus on other aspects of your financial planning, confident that your taxes are in capable hands.

Finding the right tax advisor is crucial to reaping these benefits. Start by evaluating their credentials and experience. Look for certifications such as Certified Public Accountant (CPA) or Enrolled Agent (EA), which indicate a solid foundation in tax law and a commitment to continuing education. Experience is equally important; an advisor with a proven track record can offer insights honed through years of practice. Client testimonials and reviews can provide additional perspective, offering firsthand accounts of the advisor's expertise and customer service. These reviews serve as a testament to the advisor's ability to deliver results and build trust with clients. By considering these factors, you can select a professional who aligns with your specific needs and financial objectives.

In today's digital age, technology has revolutionized the way we access personalized tax advice. Virtual tax consultation services offer convenience and flexibility, allowing you to connect with advisors from the comfort of your home. These platforms often provide tailored solutions based on your input, using algorithms to generate personalized recommendations. This approach can be particularly beneficial for those with straightforward tax situations or for initial consultations. Additionally, many services offer video conferencing, enabling face-to-face interaction with advisors without the need for in-person meetings. This digital connectivity ensures that expert advice is accessible regardless of your location and can be a valuable supplement to traditional advisory services. By leveraging these technological advances, you can enhance your tax planning strategy with ease and efficiency.

6.6 Leveraging Technology for Tax Efficiency

In today's digital age, technology has become a vital ally in managing taxes, transforming what was once a cumbersome task into a streamlined process. Imagine having a personal assistant who handles the tedious aspects of tax preparation—all thanks to automated expense tracking apps. These apps meticulously categorize and track expenses throughout the year, ensuring you never lose track of deductible costs. They allow you to snap a photo of a receipt, instantly storing it for future reference. This real-time tracking not only saves time but also increases accuracy, reducing the risk of overlooking expenses that could lower your tax bill. By embracing these tools, you can focus on what truly matters, using technology to handle the details.

When it comes to tax software, the market offers a wide range of options designed to meet various needs. TurboTax and TaxSlayer stand out as popular choices, each providing unique features that cater to different filing situations. TurboTax is renowned for its user-friendly interface and comprehensive guidance, making it ideal for those with complex tax scenarios. It offers live assistance from tax experts and ensures that every deduction and credit is explored. On the other hand, TaxSlayer appeals to budget-conscious filers, offering straightforward navigation and real-time tax result updates at a competitive price. Both platforms integrate seamlessly with financial accounts, pulling in data automatically to minimize manual entry errors. For those who prefer the convenience of mobile apps, options like Cash App Taxes make filing on the go simple and efficient. These apps are designed with the user in mind, featuring intuitive layouts and step-by-step instructions that simplify the filing process.

The advantages of using technology for tax management extend beyond simple convenience. Real-time updates and alerts keep you informed of important deadlines and changes in tax laws, allowing you to adjust your strategy proactively. For instance, if a new deduction becomes available, your tax software can alert you, ensuring you take full advantage of the change. Integration with financial accounts means your tax software can access and organize relevant data with minimal input from you, enhancing accuracy and reducing the chance of errors. This level of organization is invaluable, particularly when managing multiple income streams or complex deductions. By centralizing your financial information, technology helps you maintain a clear overview of your tax situation, fostering a sense of control and preparedness.

Choosing the right technological tools for your tax needs requires careful consideration. It's essential to select software that aligns with your specific financial requirements. Look for user-friendly interfaces that simplify navigation and offer clear instructions. An intuitive layout can make a significant difference, especially for those who might find tax filing intimidating. Additionally, consider the level of customer support available. Access to knowledgeable support staff can be a lifesaver if you encounter challenges or need clarification on certain aspects of your return. Whether through live chat, phone support, or comprehensive FAQs, robust support services can enhance your confidence and ensure a smooth filing experience.

As we wrap up this chapter on overcoming tax challenges and fears, remember that technology is more than just a tool—it's a partner in your financial journey. By integrating digital solutions into your tax strategy, you empower yourself to navigate the complexities of tax filing with ease and precision. This chapter has equipped you with the knowledge to harness these tools effectively, setting the stage for a more informed and proactive approach to managing your taxes. In the next chapter, we will explore how to build long-term financial strategies that align with your tax planning efforts, ensuring a secure and prosperous future.

Don't move on to the next chapter without doing the following;

1. Have you created a folder where you store all your receipts and paper-work? I may sound repetitive here, but it's necessary
2. Have you downloaded one of the free spreadsheets? Go to https://www.shoeboxed.com/blog/tax-expense-spreadsheet/ to check out the recommendations
3. Have you chosen what software you will use? Check out IRS Free File, Cash App Taxes, or TaxSlayer. You only need this if you're going to file yourself, otherwise, if you will file through an accountant, they'll use their own software
4. If you have a more complicated tax position, have you chosen who could help you? Get recommendations from friends or family, or go to www.cpafinder.com and enter your zip code
5. Do you want to subscribe to podcasts, webinars, or newsletters? Pick a couple and read/listen to them each month

Chapter 7

Building Long-Term Financial Strategies

Imagine retirement as a long-awaited vacation, one that requires thoughtful planning and preparation to ensure it's enjoyed to the fullest. Just as you wouldn't embark on a journey without a map or itinerary, you shouldn't approach retirement without a solid, tax-efficient strategy. This chapter delves into the art of aligning tax planning with retirement goals, providing the tools needed to navigate the complexities of retirement savings, withdrawals, and tax implications.

7.1 Aligning Tax Planning with Retirement Goals

Retirement planning is more than just setting aside money; it's about strategically managing your assets and their tax implications to ensure financial security. One critical aspect is understanding how different retirement account withdrawals affect your taxes. Withdrawals from traditional IRAs and 401(k)s are taxed as ordinary income, which can push you into a higher tax bracket if you're still earning when you withdraw. This makes it crucial to plan withdrawals carefully, especially when considering Required Minimum Distributions (RMDs). Once you reach age 73, you're required to start taking

RMDs from these accounts, and those withdrawals add to your taxable income. By strategically managing your RMDs, such as taking withdrawals earlier or considering qualified charitable distributions, you can potentially reduce the tax impact.

The decision to convert a traditional IRA to a Roth IRA is another strategic move that can significantly influence your retirement tax landscape. A Roth conversion involves paying taxes on the converted amount now to enjoy tax-free growth and withdrawals later. This strategy can be particularly beneficial if you anticipate being in a higher tax bracket in the future. Please get advice before doing this from a financial planner. There is a great article in the references section: "Is a Roth IRA conversion right for you?" By converting in lower-income years, you can minimize the tax hit, allowing your investments to grow tax-free. Moreover, Roth IRAs don't require RMDs, offering greater flexibility and control over your retirement funds. Timing is key; consider partial conversions to manage your tax bracket effectively, spreading the tax liability over several years to lessen the burden.

Balancing pre-tax and after-tax contributions is essential to optimize your retirement savings. Traditional IRAs and 401(k)s offer immediate tax savings through pre-tax contributions, reducing your current taxable income. However, withdrawals in retirement are taxed. Conversely, Roth accounts are funded with after-tax dollars, meaning your contributions don't reduce your current tax bill, but withdrawals are tax-free. This balance allows you to diversify your tax exposure, providing flexibility to draw from different accounts depending on your tax situation in retirement. The decision often hinges on your current and expected future tax brackets, requiring careful consideration of your long-term financial goals.

To minimize taxes in retirement, consider employing tax-efficient with-drawal sequences. This strategy involves planning, which accounts to draw down first to optimize tax efficiency. Typically, it's advantageous to withdraw from taxable accounts first, allowing tax-advantaged accounts to continue growing. This approach not only stretches your retirement savings but also helps manage your taxable income and potential Social Security benefit taxation. Additionally, strategic withdrawals from tax-deferred accounts, coupled with Roth conversions, can further optimize your tax position. Engaging a financial advisor to tailor these strategies to your specific circumstances can enhance their effectiveness, ensuring that your retirement years are financially secure. You don't need to be an expert in this field, just enough to keep you informed. I whole a whole other book called "Retirement Planning Made Easy," So if planning for your retirement is of interest, be sure to pick up a copy.

Case Study: Crafting a Tax-Efficient Retirement Plan

Consider Jane, a retiree who strategically planned her withdrawals. By converting a portion of her traditional IRA to a Roth IRA each year, she minimized her future RMDs and tax liability. She also staggered withdrawals from her taxable accounts, allowing her Roth IRA to grow untouched. This approach ensured a steady income while keeping her tax bracket manageable, showcasing the power of informed tax planning in retirement.

7.2 Tax-Efficient Wealth-Building Techniques

When you think about building wealth, consider how taxes play a pivotal role in how much of your earnings you actually keep. Tax-efficient investing is about making smart choices that minimize the taxes you pay, allowing your wealth to grow more effectively. For instance, certain funds, like those with low turnover rates, can significantly reduce taxable events. Exchange-traded funds (ETFs), known for their tax efficiency, are a great example. They generally incur fewer capital gains distributions compared to mutual funds, meaning you potentially pay less in taxes each year. By carefully selecting where you invest, you can keep more of your gains working for you rather than handing them over to the tax authorities.

Tax-advantaged accounts are another cornerstone of wealth-building. These accounts, such as Health Savings Accounts (HSAs), offer unique benefits that go beyond traditional savings. HSAs, for instance, provide a triple tax advantage: contributions are tax-deductible, the account grows tax-free, and withdrawals for qualified medical expenses are not taxed. This makes HSAs not just a tool for covering healthcare costs but a powerful investment vehicle. By contributing to an HSA and allowing it to grow, you can accumulate a significant sum that can be used in retirement, either for medical expenses or, after age 65, for any purpose with a tax similar to an IRA. This dual-purpose utility enhances both your health and financial security.

Diversification in your investment portfolio is crucial, but tax diversification is equally important. By spreading your investments across taxable, tax-deferred, and tax-free accounts, you can manage your tax liabilities more effectively. Tax diversification provides flexibility, allowing you to choose which accounts to draw from based on your current tax situation. For example, during high-income years, you might rely more on withdrawals from Roth accounts, which are tax-free, while in lower-income years, you could benefit from tapping into tax-deferred accounts. This strategy helps in optimizing your tax bill over the long term, maximizing the amount of money you retain as you build and manage your wealth.

Managing investment income tax efficiently involves understanding the different tax treatments of dividends and interest. Qualified dividends, which meet specific IRS requirements, are taxed at the lower capital gains rates, unlike ordinary dividends taxed at higher income rates. This distinction can save you a significant amount in taxes, making it wise to consider investments that yield qualified dividends. Municipal bonds present another tax-efficient option, as the interest earned is typically exempt from federal taxes and, in some cases, state and local taxes as well. This allows you to earn interest tax-free, making them particularly attractive to investors in higher tax brackets. By focusing on these tax-efficient income streams, you can reduce your taxable income and enhance your investment returns.

Strategically managing your investments with tax efficiency in mind is not just for the wealthy; it's a practical approach for anyone looking to maximize their financial health. By understanding and implementing strategies such as investing in tax-efficient funds, leveraging tax-advantaged accounts, diversifying tax exposure, and minimizing taxes on investment income, you set yourself on a path to more sustainable wealth accumulation. These strategies are tools that, when used wisely, can greatly enhance your financial freedom and security, allowing you to focus on what matters most to you without the constant worry of tax burdens chipping away at your progress.

7.3 Incorporating Estate Planning into Tax Strategy

Estate planning might sound like something only the ultra-wealthy need, but it's a vital tool for anyone looking to secure their financial legacy. Effective estate planning minimizes estate taxes and preserves wealth for future generations. At the heart of this process is understanding federal estate tax exemption limits, which determine how much of your estate is exempt from taxes upon your passing. As of 2024, each individual can pass up to $12.92 million tax-free, a figure that is subject to change based on legislation. This exemption allows you to shield a significant portion of your assets from hefty federal estate taxes. However, staying informed about these limits is crucial, as they can fluctuate with changes in tax laws. Regularly reviewing your estate plan can ensure you're making the most of these exemptions, preserving more of your wealth for your heirs.

Trusts are powerful tools in estate planning, offering flexibility and tax benefits that can help manage estate taxes effectively. Revocable trusts allow you to retain control over your assets during your lifetime, with the ability to modify terms as needed. They don't offer immediate tax benefits, but they ensure a smooth transfer of assets to your beneficiaries, avoiding the probate process. Irrevocable trusts, on the other hand, provide immediate tax advantages. Once assets are placed in an irrevocable trust, they are removed from your taxable estate, which can significantly reduce estate taxes. However, you relinquish control over these assets. Both types of trusts serve distinct purposes and can be tailored to fit your financial goals and family needs. Using trusts strategically can help manage your estate taxes and maintain control over how your assets are distributed.

Gifting strategies offer another avenue for reducing estate taxes. The annual gift tax exclusion is a powerful tool, allowing you to give up to $17,000 per recipient per year tax-free in 2024. These gifts reduce the size of your taxable estate, effectively transferring wealth to your beneficiaries while avoiding gift and estate taxes. Over time, this strategy can significantly reduce your estate tax liability. Consider using these gifts to support family members, fund educational expenses, or even contribute to a loved one's retirement. It's a way to see the impact of your generosity while also benefiting your estate plan. Thoughtful gifting can ensure that more of your wealth reaches the people and causes you care about rather than being eroded by taxes.

Estate planning is not a set-it-and-forget-it task. Regular updates are crucial to ensure your plans align with current tax laws and your personal circumstances. Tax legislation changes can alter the effectiveness of your strategies, necessitating adjustments to your estate plan. Additionally, life events such as marriages, births, or changes in financial status should prompt a review. An outdated estate plan can lead to unintended tax consequences or even disputes among heirs. By periodically revisiting your estate plan, you can adapt to new laws and life changes, ensuring your wishes are honored and your financial legacy is preserved. Engaging with a financial advisor or estate planning attorney can provide guidance and peace of mind, ensuring your estate plan remains effective and aligned with your goals.

Maintaining a proactive stance on your estate plan can empower you to take control of your financial future. By understanding the tax implications and utilizing trusts and gifting strategies, you can minimize tax liabilities while maximizing the impact of your wealth. Regular reviews ensure your plan evolves with the changing landscape, protecting your legacy and providing security for your heirs.

Estate planning is complex and not to be taken lightly. I have a whole other book on this called "Estate Planning Made Easy." If planning for the next generation is important to you and you want to preserve as much of your wealth for your family, then you should definitely grab a copy.

7.4 The Role of Tax Planning in Financial Independence

Picture financial independence as the freedom to live life on your own terms without the constraints of financial worry. At its core, financial independence is about having enough savings, investments, and income streams to cover your living expenses without relying on traditional employment. Tax planning plays a pivotal role in this journey by strategically reducing tax burdens, thereby increasing your ability to save and invest more of your hard-earned money. When you minimize taxes, you maximize your savings potential, accelerating your path to financial freedom. This approach allows you to redirect funds toward investments that generate passive income, creating a cycle of growth and security that supports your independence.

The FIRE movement, standing for Financial Independence, Retire Early, embodies the principles of achieving financial independence at a younger age. This movement emphasizes aggressive saving and investing, often aiming for a savings rate of 50% or more of one's income. Within the FIRE framework, tax strategies become crucial tools for maximizing savings and managing withdrawals efficiently. Tax-efficient withdrawal strategies are key for early retirees, who often rely on a combination of taxable accounts, tax-deferred accounts, and tax-free accounts. By strategically withdrawing from these accounts, you can manage your taxable income and avoid unnecessary taxes. For instance, drawing from taxable accounts first can allow tax-deferred accounts to grow longer, potentially reducing your tax bill over time. This careful orchestration of withdrawals helps maintain the balance between enjoying your retirement and preserving your nest egg.

Passive income streams are a cornerstone of financial independence, providing a steady flow of money without the direct exchange of time for dollars. Rental properties, dividend-paying stocks, and interest from bonds are common sources. Rental income, in particular, offers significant tax benefits. Expenses like mortgage interest, property taxes, and maintenance costs can be deducted, effectively reducing the taxable income from your rental properties. Additionally, depreciation provides another layer of tax efficiency, allowing you to write off a portion of the property's value each year. By optimizing these income streams for tax efficiency, you retain more of your earnings, reinforcing your financial independence and providing a cushion against unexpected expenses.

Integrating tax planning into your financial independence goals involves a comprehensive approach that aligns with your long-term vision. Start by setting clear financial goals and developing a budget that prioritizes saving and investing. Consider attending budgeting and tax planning workshops to gain practical skills and insights. These workshops can offer valuable guidance on creating a personalized financial plan that incorporates tax strategies tailored to your situation. Tools like online calculators and budgeting apps can further assist in tracking your progress and adjusting your strategies as needed. I like You Need a Budget (YNAB) and Empower. By maintaining a proactive approach and regularly revisiting your financial plan, you ensure that your tax planning efforts remain aligned with your evolving goals. This discipline not only accelerates your journey toward financial independence but also enhances your overall financial literacy, equipping you with the knowledge and confidence to make informed decisions.

7.5 Passing on Wealth Through Tax-Efficient Means

Transferring wealth to the next generation often feels like navigating a complex maze, but strategic planning can help you find the right path while minimizing tax burdens. One effective method is through the use of life insurance policies. These policies are not just about providing a financial safety net; they also serve as a tax-efficient tool for wealth transfer. When structured properly, life insurance can ensure that the payout is free from federal income taxes, providing your heirs with a lump sum that can be used to cover estate taxes or other obligations. This allows your loved ones to receive the full benefit of your legacy without being burdened by additional financial stress.

Charitable remainder trusts (CRTs) present another avenue for tax-efficient wealth transfer. By placing assets into a CRT, you can receive income for a set number of years or for life, with the remainder going to a charity of your choice. This not only provides a steady income stream but also offers immediate tax benefits, such as a charitable deduction based on the trust's value. CRTs can be particularly appealing if you have highly appreciated assets, as they allow you to bypass capital gains taxes while supporting causes you care about. This dual benefit of income generation and charitable giving makes CRTs a versatile tool in your estate planning arsenal.

Educational savings accounts, like 529 plans, are powerful tools for building a legacy through education. These accounts offer tax-advantaged growth, with contributions growing tax-free as long as they are used for qualified educational expenses. By investing in a 529 plan, you not only support a child's educational journey but also reduce your taxable estate. Many states offer additional tax benefits for contributions, making 529 plans a compelling choice for those looking to pass on their wealth while fostering future opportunities for their descendants. This approach ensures that your legacy is not just financial but also educational, empowering the next generation with the gift of learning.

Family limited partnerships (FLPs) offer a sophisticated method for trans-ferring wealth while maintaining control over assets. By placing family assets into an FLP, you can gift partnership interests to your heirs at a discounted valuation. This takes advantage of valuation discounts for lack of control and marketability, effectively reducing the taxable value of the gift. FLPs also allow you to retain management control, ensuring assets are handled according to your wishes. This structure not only facilitates tax-efficient wealth transfer but also strengthens family bonds by involving multiple generations in the management of family assets.

Clear communication remains the cornerstone of successful succession planning. It's essential to engage in open and honest discussions with your family about your estate plans. Regular family meetings can serve as a platform to share your goals and intentions, ensuring everyone is on the same page. These discussions help prevent misunderstandings and conflicts, fostering a sense of unity and shared purpose. By involving your family in the planning process, you create a legacy of transparency and collaboration, ensuring your wealth is passed on according to your wishes.

7.6 Continuous Learning in Tax and Financial Planning

In a world where tax laws change as regularly as the seasons, staying informed is like having a reliable compass guiding you through financial landscapes. These evolving regulations can have profound effects on your finances, from how much you owe to the strategies that best protect your assets. Ignoring these changes is like ignoring weather forecasts when planning a trip—you might get caught in a storm of unexpected tax bills or missed opportunities for savings. Staying updated on tax laws is crucial because even small amendments can impact your deductions, credits, and overall financial strategy. For instance, a shift in tax bracket thresholds might mean the difference between paying thousands more or saving money. This underscores the importance of continuous education, not just for keeping up but for actively shaping your financial future. If you subscribed to updates or newsletters in Chapter 6, you should get these updates through those sources.

To stay on top of these changes, consider leveraging a variety of resources tailored to enhance your financial literacy. Online courses and webinars are excellent tools for diving into specific topics at your own pace. Platforms like Coursera or edX offer courses taught by experts, providing deep insights into complex tax topics. Meanwhile, industry journals and books provide comprehensive overviews and analyses, keeping you informed on broader economic trends and legislative changes. These resources serve as both a foundation and a continual update to your understanding, ensuring that your knowledge grows alongside the shifting financial landscape.

Participation in tax and financial planning communities can further enrich your learning experience. Online forums and groups, such as those found on Reddit or LinkedIn, offer platforms for discussing the latest tax updates and strategies. These communities are invaluable for sharing experiences, asking questions, and learning from others' successes and mistakes. Engaging with these groups not only enhances your understanding but also builds a network of support that can provide guidance and encouragement. The collective wisdom of these communities can offer insights that might not be readily available elsewhere, making them a vital component of your educational toolkit.

Taking a proactive approach to financial education is about setting personal learning goals and committing to regular review sessions. Scheduling time to assess your financial situation and strategies ensures that you remain aligned with your goals and responsive to any changes. Consider setting quarterly or biannual meetings with yourself—or with a financial advisor—to evaluate your progress and adjust your plans. This habit of regular review fosters a mindset of continuous improvement, helping you anticipate challenges and seize opportunities ahead of time. Such proactive habits not only enhance your financial literacy but also build confidence in your ability to manage your finances effectively.

As you weave these practices into your routine, remember that financial education is a lifelong endeavor. The more informed you are, the more empowered you'll feel in making decisions that impact your financial well-being. Staying curious and engaged with your financial education ensures that you are always prepared for whatever changes come your way, allowing you to navigate the financial world with assurance and agility. In the next chapter, we will explore tools and resources that can further support your financial planning, offering practical aids to complement the knowledge you've gained.

Don't move on to the next chapter without doing the following;

1. Do you need to get tax advice on your retirement accounts?
2. Do you need to begin estate planning? If you have children, you must have a will. It's a whole separate topic, but is something that is fiscally responsible to have done
3. Do you need long-term tax planning for your wealth building? Get advice

and then have regular check-in meetings to track your progress
4. Subscribe, if you haven't already to newsletters or updates you can read to keep yourself informed

Chapter 8

Interactive Tools and Resources

Imagine you're embarking on a road trip, the open highway before you brimming with potential destinations. Your GPS serves as your guide, offering directions to ensure you reach your goals efficiently and without unnecessary detours. In the realm of personal taxes, think of worksheets as your financial GPS—tools designed to navigate the complex landscape of tax planning with precision and confidence. These worksheets are invaluable when it comes to customizing your tax strategies to suit your unique financial situation, much like how a tailored map enhances a journey.

Personalized tax planning worksheets function as a dynamic framework, allowing you to track your income and expenses with clarity and accuracy. By structuring your financial information in a systematic way, these worksheets enable you to identify potential deductions and credits that align with your specific circumstances. They serve as a living document, adapting to changes in your financial life and ensuring that your tax strategy remains relevant and optimized. This adaptability is crucial, as it allows you to adjust your planning in response to shifts such as a new job, a significant purchase, or changes in tax laws.

To effectively utilize these worksheets, you'll want to start with a solid foundation. Begin by gathering all relevant financial documents, including pay stubs, receipts, and bank statements. Use these to populate customizable fields within your worksheets, which should include categories for income, expenses, deductions, and credits. By breaking down your financial information into these segments, you can see a clearer picture of your overall financial health and pinpoint areas where you might increase efficiency or seize new opportunities.

Ready-to-use templates can make this process even smoother. For instance, the Mod Boutique Agency's monthly expense tracker is perfect for independent contractors. It automatically calculates monthly expenses and provides totals for potential tax deductions. Alternatively, the Keeper Tax Office Deduction Template is tailored for home office deductions, offering a business-use percentage calculator to optimize write-offs. These templates, freely available online, cater to various needs and simplify the process of financial tracking by providing a structured format that you can easily adapt to your needs. For a list of the top templates, go to References at the back of the book and go to Tax Expense Spreadsheet: Top 5 Free Templates.

When using worksheets for strategic tax planning, follow a step-by-step approach. Begin by logging all sources of income, ensuring you account for every dollar earned. Next, meticulously track expenses, categorizing them in line with potential deductions. This detailed record-keeping is vital for identifying eligible deductions and credits, such as those for charitable contributions or educational expenses. By projecting your annual tax liabilities, you can better plan for the year ahead, setting aside the necessary funds to cover your tax obligations without stress or last-minute scrambles.

Regular updates and reviews of your worksheet data are not just advisable; they are essential. Financial situations can change rapidly, and staying on top of these changes ensures that your tax planning remains accurate and effective. Set aside time each quarter to review and update your financial summaries, adjusting for any new developments. This regular maintenance prevents discrepancies and ensures that you are always working with the most current information.

Exercise: Quarterly Financial Check-in

Allocate time each quarter to sit down with your worksheets. Review your income and expenses, ensuring all entries are up-to-date. Identify any new deductions or credits that may have arisen and update your projections accordingly. This practice keeps your financial strategy aligned with your life, ensuring that no opportunities are missed.

8.1 Using Online Calculators to Estimate Tax Liabilities

Imagine a tool that takes the guesswork out of taxes, providing clarity and precision with just a few clicks. Online tax calculators do just that, offering a convenient and accurate way to estimate your tax liabilities. These digital tools streamline the process, allowing you to input key financial data and instantly receive a detailed breakdown of what you might owe or expect as a refund. This convenience is invaluable, particularly when you're juggling multiple financial responsibilities. Calculators eliminate the need for cumbersome manual calculations, ensuring that you don't overlook any critical details that could impact your financial picture. This is only relevant if you're self-employed.

Several popular options stand out for their user-friendly interfaces and comprehensive features. The IRS tax withholding estimator, for example, is designed to help you determine how much tax should be withheld from your paycheck. By adjusting your withholdings, you can better manage your take-home pay and avoid surprises come tax season. For those who are self-employed, specialized calculators can estimate quarterly tax payments, ensuring you stay on top of your obligations and avoid penalties. These tools cater to different needs, allowing you to choose one that aligns with your specific financial situation.

Choosing the right calculator is crucial to maximizing its benefits. Look for features that suit your needs, such as the ability to input diverse income sources, deductions, and credits. A good calculator will also provide explanations for its calculations, helping you understand the underlying factors that influence your tax liability. This transparency not only aids in planning but also empowers you to make informed decisions about your finances. With the right tool, you can simulate various scenarios, such as potential changes in income or deductions, and see how these adjustments impact your overall tax picture.

Consider several scenarios where calculators prove particularly useful. For freelancers and gig workers, estimating quarterly self-employment taxes can be a daunting task. A dedicated calculator simplifies this process, allowing you to input your income and expenses and receive an estimate of what you owe. Suggested software to use could be TaxSlayer or Cash App Taxes. This foresight helps you budget more effectively and prevents unexpected tax bills. Similarly, if you're planning for retirement, calculators can project potential contributions to retirement accounts. By entering your current savings and expected growth rates, these tools can estimate how much you'll need to contribute to reach your retirement goals, all while considering tax implications.

Visualizing your tax situation through these digital aids not only brings peace of mind but also enhances your financial strategy. By regularly using calculators, you gain a clearer understanding of your tax obligations and how they fit into the broader context of your financial life. If you're planning a major life change, such as buying a home or starting a business, calculators can provide valuable insights into the potential tax impact. This foresight allows you to plan proactively, ensuring that you make decisions that align with your long-term financial objectives.

Interactive Element: Try It Yourself

Visit the NerdWallet Tax Calculator and input your income, age, and filing status. Observe how these variables affect your estimated federal taxes. Experiment with different scenarios, such as adjusting your income or deductions, to see how your tax liability changes. This hands-on approach helps reinforce your understanding and aids in strategic planning.

8.2 Interactive Checklists for Tax Season Readiness

Imagine standing in your garage, surrounded by tools and parts, ready to tackle a DIY project. Without a plan, you might find yourself overwhelmed, unsure of where to start or what to do next. This is where a checklist becomes invaluable, guiding you through each step with clarity and purpose. In the realm of taxes, an interactive checklist serves a similar function, transforming the often-daunting task of tax preparation into a structured, manageable process. These checklists provide step-by-step guidance, ensuring that you have all your bases covered, from gathering documents to filing your return.

An effective tax season checklist acts as your road map, helping you navigate the various tasks involved in preparing your taxes. Start with a pre-filing document checklist, which includes gathering W-2s, 1099s, and receipts for deductible expenses. This initial step ensures that you have all the necessary documentation before diving into calculations and forms. Next, consider creating an audit preparation checklist. This might involve organizing past returns, keeping detailed records of deductions, and maintaining correspondence with the IRS. By having these documents readily available, you not only ease the filing process but also prepare yourself for potential audits, reducing stress and uncertainty.

The benefits of using checklists extend beyond mere organization. They play a crucial role in reducing stress and enhancing efficiency during tax season. By following a checklist, you minimize the risk of overlooking important details, such as missed deductions or credits, which can significantly impact your final tax bill. This organized approach not only saves time but also increases accuracy, ensuring that your tax return is complete and compliant. With a well-structured checklist, you can approach tax season with confidence, knowing that you have a clear plan in place to tackle each task methodically.

Creating personalized checklists tailored to your unique tax situation requires some thought and planning. Start by considering your specific financial circumstances. Are you a business owner with complex deductions? Or perhaps a freelancer with multiple income streams? Whatever your situation, tailor your checklist to include tasks and reminders relevant to your needs. Incorporate deadlines for quarterly estimated payments, reminders for retirement contributions, and notes on any new tax laws that may affect you. By customizing your checklist, you ensure that it aligns with your financial goals and obligations, minimizing the chance of oversight.

As you develop your checklist, remember to incorporate deadlines and reminders that keep you on track. Set calendar alerts for important dates, such as tax filing deadlines or quarterly payments. This proactive approach prevents last-minute scrambles and helps you manage your time effectively. Additionally, consider using digital tools or apps that offer interactive check-lists. These platforms often provide features like automatic reminders, shared access for collaboration, and integration with other financial tools, further streamlining your tax preparation process.

Interactive Element: Create Your Custom Tax Checklist

Take a moment to draft your personalized tax checklist. List tasks specific to your situation and set deadlines for each. Use digital tools to create reminders and share your checklist with a trusted advisor for additional input. This practice builds a tailored road map, ensuring a smooth and stress-free tax season. Your checklist should include all your sources of income, your deductions, and your expenses.

8.3 Building a Supportive Tax Strategy Community

Imagine being part of a group where everyone speaks the same language of numbers and deductions, where the goal is mutual support and shared success in navigating the tax landscape. Engaging with a tax strategy community offers immense value, not just in the form of shared experiences but also through the collective wisdom that comes from diverse backgrounds and perspectives. Within these communities, you find people who have faced similar tax challenges and can offer insights and strategies that you might not have considered. By participating, you tap into a wealth of knowledge that can help demystify complex tax issues and provide reassurance that you're not alone in facing them.

Online forums and social media groups serve as vibrant meeting places for these discussions. Consider exploring platforms like Reddit, where tax-focused communities share advice, answer questions, and discuss the latest changes in tax laws. A subreddit dedicated to personal finance or taxes can be a treasure trove of tips and anecdotes from individuals who have successfully navigated their tax situations. Similarly, LinkedIn hosts groups where professionals discuss strategies, share articles, and network with others in the field. These platforms provide a space to connect with like-minded individuals and experts who can offer guidance and support.

Active participation in these communities can greatly enhance your understanding and confidence in managing your taxes. By contributing to discussions, you not only learn but also teach, reinforcing your own knowledge. Asking questions is a powerful way to clarify doubts and gain different perspectives. Offering advice, even on topics you're familiar with, can strengthen your grasp on those subjects and build your reputation within the community. This exchange of information fosters a sense of belonging and camaraderie, turning the often solitary task of tax planning into a collaborative effort.

The benefits of community engagement are numerous, as evidenced by success stories from participants. Take the case of Clara, a self-employed graphic designer who joined a Reddit tax community. Through her interactions, she learned about a deduction she had previously overlooked, significantly reducing her tax liability and increasing the amount of money she retained in her business. Her experience inspired her to contribute more actively, sharing her journey and helping others avoid similar oversights. This mutual exchange not only saved her money but also gave her the confidence to tackle her taxes with newfound expertise.

Building a supportive tax strategy community isn't just about accessing information; it's about creating connections that empower you to make informed financial decisions. These communities are dynamic environments where you can stay updated on tax trends, learn about new tools, and develop strategies tailored to your needs. The relationships you build can become invaluable resources, offering support during tax season and beyond. Embrace the opportunity to engage, and you'll find that the collective knowledge of a community can transform your approach to taxes, making the process less daunting and more manageable.

8.4 Engaging with Financial Education Platforms

Imagine having a personal tutor who guides you through the complexities of taxes, breaking down intricate concepts into digestible lessons. Financial education platforms offer this kind of support, providing a wealth of resources that deepen your understanding of tax-related matters. These platforms are treasure troves of knowledge, offering courses, webinars, and interactive content designed to enhance your financial literacy. With structured lessons and expert insights, you can gain a clearer picture of the tax landscape, empowering you to make informed decisions that align with your financial goals.

Let's explore some reputable platforms that provide tax-related content. Khan Academy is well-known for its comprehensive approach to financial literacy, offering free courses that cover a wide range of topics, including taxes. Their lessons are designed to cater to different learning styles, using a mix of video tutorials, articles, and practice exercises to reinforce understanding. On the other hand, Coursera provides more specialized courses, often in partnership with universities and organizations. These courses delve into various aspects of tax law and financial planning, providing in-depth knowledge that can be applied to real-world scenarios. By accessing these platforms, you can tailor your learning experience to suit your needs, selecting courses that align with your interests and skill level.

Diversity in learning formats is essential for maintaining engagement and ensuring that new concepts are absorbed effectively. Video tutorials offer a visual and auditory learning experience, making complex topics more accessible. They allow you to see concepts in action, with real-world examples and step-by-step guides that clarify each point. Interactive quizzes, on the other hand, provide a hands-on approach to learning, allowing you to test your knowledge and receive immediate feedback. This interactive element helps reinforce learning, ensuring that new information is retained. By exploring different formats, you can find the approach that resonates most with you, enhancing your understanding and confidence in managing your taxes.

Continuous learning through these platforms is not just about acquiring new skills; it's about staying informed and adaptable in a constantly changing tax environment. Tax laws and regulations evolve, and keeping up-to-date is crucial for effective tax management. By regularly engaging with educational content, you can anticipate changes and adapt your strategies accordingly. This proactive approach ensures that you remain compliant and take advantage of new opportunities, such as tax credits or deductions, that may arise. Staying informed not only protects you from potential pitfalls but also positions you to optimize your financial situation, ensuring that you're always making the most of the resources available to you.

8.5 Resources for Ongoing Tax Education and Updates

Staying informed about the ever-evolving world of tax laws is paramount for effective tax management. With tax reforms and updates occurring regularly, it's easy to feel overwhelmed by the sheer volume of information. However, understanding these changes is crucial as they can directly impact your financial decisions, influencing everything from the deductions you can claim to the credits you might qualify for. To ensure you're always in the know, it's wise to tap into reliable resources that offer up-to-date information and insights.

Start with the IRS website—a cornerstone of tax information. It provides a wealth of resources, including publications, forms, and detailed explanations of tax laws. The IRS regularly updates its site to reflect the latest tax code changes, making it a trustworthy source for accurate information. For instance, you can find guidance on new tax credits and deductions, keeping you equipped to make the most of any benefits available. The IRS also offers an Interactive Tax Assistant, a helpful tool that answers questions and clarifies complex tax topics, allowing you to navigate the intricacies of the tax system with greater confidence.

In addition to official sources, subscribing to tax-focused newsletters can be incredibly beneficial. These publications often provide analysis and commentary on the latest tax developments, breaking down complex topics into digestible pieces. Subscriptions to these newsletters mean you'll receive regular updates directly to your inbox, ensuring you're always aware of any significant changes that might affect your tax strategy. Look for newsletters from reputable financial organizations or tax professionals who have a track record of delivering insightful, timely information.

Blogs dedicated to tax policy are another excellent resource for staying informed. These blogs delve into the nuances of tax law, offering perspectives and interpretations that can enhance your understanding. Many of these blogs are written by experts who provide in-depth analysis and practical advice, helping you apply new knowledge to your personal financial situation. By engaging with this content, you can stay ahead of the curve, anticipating changes and adjusting your strategies accordingly.

Technology also plays a vital role in keeping you informed. Mobile apps designed for tax alerts and news provide real-time updates on tax matters, ensuring you never miss a critical development. These apps often allow you to customize notifications based on your interests or needs, providing a tailored flow of information that keeps you informed without overwhelming you. Additionally, some apps offer features like calculators and planning tools, integrating educational content with practical applications to support your tax management efforts.

The importance of staying current with tax developments cannot be over-stated. New tax credits and deductions can significantly affect your financial planning, offering opportunities to save money or optimize your tax position. For example, understanding how recent changes to retirement account contribution limits might impact your savings strategy is essential for effective planning. By maintaining a constant flow of information from trusted sources, you can ensure your tax strategies are always aligned with current laws, maximizing your financial potential.

Incorporating these resources into your routine doesn't require a major time commitment. A few minutes each week spent reviewing updates or reading a newsletter can keep you informed and prepared. This proactive approach not only aids in immediate tax planning but also lays the groundwork for long-term financial success. By staying educated, you empower yourself to make informed decisions, adapt to changes with ease, and ensure that your tax strategy is both compliant and optimized for your unique circumstances. With these tools at your disposal, you're well-equipped to navigate the complexities of taxes and achieve your financial goals.

Don't move on to the next chapter without doing the following;

1. If you haven't already, choose a tracking template or tool that you can use to track your income and expenses
2. If you haven't already, subscribe to newsletters or forums you think could be useful and set aside time once a month to review them

Conclusion

As we conclude our journey through the intricate world of personal taxes, I want to remind you of the purpose that inspired this book: to empower you with the knowledge and strategies needed to navigate the tax landscape confidently. My vision has been to demystify the complexities of taxes, enabling you to make informed decisions that minimize your tax liabilities and maximize your financial well-being. There's no need for you to be a tax expert at the end of this book, just a little more knowledgeable than you were before you started reading.

Throughout these chapters, we've covered a wide range of topics, from foundational tax concepts to advanced strategies for legal tax minimization. We started by laying the groundwork, exploring tax brackets, adjusted gross income, and the basics of deductions and credits. Building on this foundation, we delved into the art of legal tax minimization, discussing strategies like the "Buy, Borrow, Die" approach, tax shelters, and the power of tax deferral.

As we progressed, we tackled the practical aspects of tax planning, offering year-round strategies and insights into tax-efficient investing. We also navigated complex scenarios, such as managing taxes with multiple income streams, understanding capital gains, and the unique challenges faced by freelancers and small business owners. Throughout, we emphasized the importance of integrating tax strategies with your long-term financial goals, from retirement planning to estate management.

I hope you've come away with several key insights that will serve you well in your financial journey. Remember that understanding your tax bracket is crucial for making informed decisions, and that leveraging legal tax strategies can significantly reduce your tax burden. Keep in mind that tax planning is an ongoing process, requiring continuous learning and adaptation as tax laws evolve.

But knowledge alone is not enough. To truly benefit from the strategies we've discussed, you must actively engage with your finances and apply these concepts to your unique situation. Embrace the power of proactive tax planning, and you'll be amazed at the impact it can have on your financial independence. Don't be afraid to start small—even minor adjustments can lead to significant savings over time.

Your financial education doesn't end with this book. Continue exploring the resources and tools we've discussed, from tax calculators to templates. Engage with tax strategy communities, both online and in-person, to learn from the experiences of others and share your own insights. And when you need personalized guidance, don't hesitate to seek the advice of qualified professionals who can help you tailor these strategies to your specific needs.

Ensure you follow through on the action steps included at the end of each chapter so you get the true value from the book. They will be your guide to how you interactively learn as you go.

As a CPA, my commitment to your financial well-being extends beyond the pages of this book. I'm grateful for the time and energy you've invested in improving your tax literacy, and I want you to know that I'm here to support you in your ongoing journey. Your success is my success, and I'm confident that the knowledge you've gained will serve you well for years to come.

I encourage you to stay connected with the community of readers who have joined you on this path. Share your experiences, your challenges, and your triumphs. Together, we can continue to learn, grow, and thrive in the face of any tax challenge that comes our way.

Thank you for entrusting me to guide you through this important aspect of your financial life. I'm honored to be a part of your journey, and I look forward to hearing about the success you'll achieve as you put these strategies into action. Remember, the power to control your financial destiny is in your hands—and with the right knowledge and tools, there's no limit to what you can achieve.

* * *

Make a Difference with Your Review

People who give without expecting anything in return live happier lives. So, let's make a difference together!

Would you help someone just like you—curious about Financial Freedom but unsure where to start?

My mission is to make Financial Freedom understandable for everyone.

But to reach more people, I need your help.

Most people choose books based on reviews. So, I'm asking you to help someone else by leaving a review.

It costs nothing and takes less than a minute but could change someone's financial journey and turn around a family's future. Your review could help...

...one more family get out of debt
   ...one parent build their emergency fund for their family
   ...one child understand money to start their life out better than they started
   ...one more person take control of their finances
   ...one more dream come true

To make a difference, simply scan the QR code below, or click on the link and leave a review:
   https://amzn.to/3S3zaY9

Emma Maxwell

References

- *Federal income tax rates and brackets* https://www.irs.gov/filing/federal-income-tax-rates-and-brackets
- *Adjusted Gross Income vs. Taxable Income Explained* https://www.joinhomebase.com/blog/adjusted-gross-income-vs-taxable-income
- *Filing status | Internal Revenue Service* https://www.irs.gov/filing/filing-status
- *Credits and deductions | Internal Revenue Service* https://www.irs.gov/credits-and-deductions
- *The Difference Between Tax Avoidance and Tax Evasion - IRS* https://apps.irs.gov/app/understandingTaxes/whys/thm01/les03/media/ws_ans_thm01_les03.pdf
- *The Buy, Borrow, Die Tax Strategy Explained* https://physiciansthrive.com/financial-planning/buy-borrow-die-tax-planning-strategy/
- *Tax Shelter: Definition, Examples, and Legal Issues* https://www.investopedia.com/terms/t/taxshelter.asp
- *Realize the potential of HSA tax benefits* https://healthaccounts.bankofamerica.com/triple-tax-savings-advantage.shtml
- *Five Tax Planning Strategies to Use All Year to Lower Taxes* https://www.kiplinger.com/taxes/tax-planning-strategies-for-all-year-to-lower-taxes
- *5 tax-efficient investment vehicles (and how to use them)* https://www.chase.com/personal/investments/learning-and-insights/article/5-tax-efficient-investment-vehicles-and-how-to-use-them
- *Simplified option for home office deduction* https://www.irs.gov/businesses/small-businesses-self-employed/simplified-option-for-home-office-deduction

- *Online Tax Calendar | Internal Revenue Service* https://www.irs.gov/busines ses/small-businesses-self-employed/online-tax-calendar
- *Tax Planning for Individuals with Multiple Sources of Income* https://www.li nkedin.com/pulse/tax-planning-individuals-multiple-sources-income-lee-cpa-ea-ctc-olzhe
- *Capital Gains Tax: What It Is, How It Works, and Current ...* https://www.inve stopedia.com/terms/c/capital_gains_tax.asp
- *The Ultimate List of 34 Tax Deductions for Self-Employed ...* https://gusto.co m/resources/articles/taxes/self-employment-tax-deductions
- *Tax Strategies: Success Stories from Real Clients* https://www.andreawardcp a.com/case-studies-of-successful-tax-strategies-real-life-examples-o f-how-effective-tax-planning-has-benefited-clients
- *How to do taxes right as a freelancer—important pitfalls ...* https://bethkobli ner.com/advice_basics/taxes-freelancer-creative/
- *Small Business Tax Credit Programs* https://home.treasury.gov/policy-issu es/coronavirus/assistance-for-small-businesses/small-business-tax-cr edit-programs
- *Maximizing Tax Benefits with Real Estate Investor ...* https://www.taxplaniq. com/blog/maximizing-tax-benefits-with-real-estate-investor-tax-str ategies
- *IRS releases 2023 Data Book describing agency's ...* https://www.irs.gov/new sroom/irs-releases-2023-data-book-describing-agencys-transformati on-through-statistics
- *IRS Free File: Do your taxes for free* https://www.irs.gov/filing/irs-free-file-do-your-taxes-for-free
- *Tax Changes for 2023-2024: What Tax Pros Need to Know* https://www.taxsl ayerpro.com/blog/post/tax-changes-for-2023
- *Best Tax Apps Of February 2025* https://www.forbes.com/advisor/taxes/bes t-tax-apps/
- *Tax-Efficient Retirement Strategies: A Comprehensive Guide* https://www.le wis.cpa/blog/tax-planning-strategies-for-retirees
- *Is a Roth IRA conversion right for you? - Vanguard* https://investor.vanguar d.com/investor-resources-education/iras/ira-roth-conversion#:~:text=

The%20benefits%20of%20a%20Roth,tax%20savings%20down%20the%20line.

- *The essential guide to estate planning and income taxes* https://rsmus.com/insights/services/private-client/estate-planning-and-income-tax-key-considerations.html
- *Tax Strategies on FIRE: Financial Independence / Retire ...* https://twosidesoffi.com/fitaxguy/
- *Tax Expense Spreadsheet: Top 5 Free Templates* https://www.shoeboxed.com/blog/tax-expense-spreadsheet/
- *Income Tax Calculator 2024-2025* https://www.nerdwallet.com/calculator/tax-calculator
- *Interactive Tax Assistant (ITA)* https://www.irs.gov/help/ita
- *NGPF Taxes Unit* https://www.ngpf.org/curriculum/taxes/

Also by Emma Maxwell

I'm proud to say this is now my fourth book. They all complement each other in the personal finance space and are great reads if you liked what you read... .check them out!

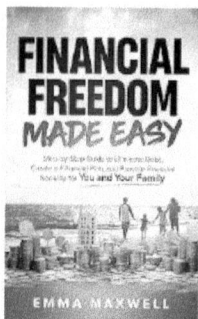

Financial Freedom Made Easy: Step-by-Step Guide to Eliminate Debt, Create a Financial Plan, and Provide Security for you and your Family
Achieve Financial Independence and Secure Your Family's Future in Just a Few Simple Steps – Even if You're Starting from Scratch

Financial Freedom Made Easy is your comprehensive, practical guide to financial independence and peace of mind.

Here's just a glimpse of what you'll discover inside:

- **6 practical steps** to create a realistic budget for your family
- The **most effective strategies** for paying off credit card debt, including the *Debt Pay Down* and *Debt Accelerator* methods
- **Emergency Fund 101**: the step-by-step process for building your family's safety net.
- **Investment basics for beginners**: Clear explanations of investing terms and key steps to get you started
- Why **low-risk investment options** can still yield significant returns
- **Easy-to-understand guidelines** for retirement planning to ensure a comfortable future
- **Simple tax planning strategies** to maximize your savings
- How to overcome the **psychological barriers** that hinder good financial habits
- **Real-life success stories** to inspire and motivate your journey
...and so much more!

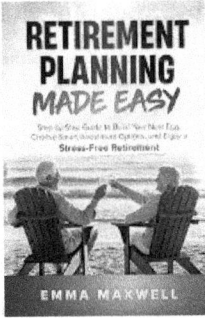

Retirement Planning Made Easy: Step-by-Step Guide to Build Your Nest Egg, Choose Smart Investment Options, and Enjoy a Stress-Free Retirement

With **Retirement Planning Made Easy**, you have a blueprint to navigate your unique financial landscape, tearing down the barriers of complex financial jargon. Inside, you'll learn:

- **How much you will need to afford to retire**, taking into account rising healthcare costs and your future income streams

- Proven strategies to **catch up on savings**, tailored specifically for late starters to ensure that no opportunity is wasted

- **Established investment options** based on your risk profile and age

- **Social Security Made Easy**: How and when to start your Social Security to optimize your retirement

- How to prepare for unpredictable **healthcare costs**, offering options for cover and the costs you may incur in your golden years

- **Debt vs. savings**: A guide to balance priorities effectively and make informed financial decisions to get you debt-free

- How to transition seamlessly to a fulfilling retirement after years in the workforce, **finding new purpose**

- The actionable steps to ensure you **never outlive your savings**, safeguarding your standard of living and independence

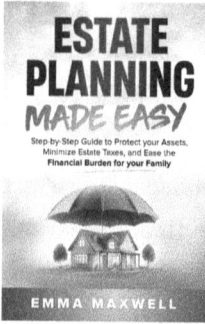

Estate Planning Made Easy: Step-by-Step Guide to Protect your Assets, Minimize Estate Taxes, and Ease the Financial Burden for your Family

With **Estate Planning Made Easy**, you'll find it's easier than you ever thought possible. This guide demystifies the often overwhelming world of estate planning.

Here's a glance at what you'll uncover in this comprehensive guide:

- **The fundamental differences between trusts and wills** and which one suits your specific needs the best.

- **A streamlined process to navigate probate** and minimize its impact on your estate.

- **Tax strategies that minimize estate taxes** and help preserve more of your wealth for your heirs.

- **Clear guidelines for selecting executors and trustees** to ensure your wishes are carried out seamlessly.

- **Detailed steps for naming guardians** to secure the future and safety of your children.

- **Expert advice on ensuring fair asset distribution** in blended families.

- Essential insights on **estate planning for business owners** to safeguard business continuity.

- The **vital role of power of attorney** and how it simplifies estate management.

- **Common estate planning pitfalls to avoid**, ensuring your plan is effective and robust.

- **Tips on selecting the right estate planning attorney** without feeling overwhelmed.

www.ingramcontent.com/pod-product-compliance
Lightning Source LLC
Chambersburg PA
CBHW071432210326
41597CB00020B/3762